£8·98

Juvenile Offending

Juvenile Offending

Prevention through Intermediate Treatment

SARAH CURTIS

B. T. Batsford Ltd · *London*

First published 1989

All rights reserved. No part of this publication
may be reproduced, in any form or by any means,
without permission from the Publisher

Typeset by Deltatype Ltd, Ellesmere Port, Cheshire
and printed in Great Britain by
Dotesios (Printers) Ltd, Trowbridge, Wilts

Published by B T Batsford Ltd
4 Fitzhardinge Street, London W1H 0AH

A CIP catalogue record for this book is
available from the British Library

ISBN 0 7134 5782 7

CONTENTS

ACKNOWLEDGEMENTS

This book could not have been written without the full co-operation of those working with young offenders and young people at risk in the six areas I visited. My first, warm thanks must go to them for giving me their valuable time, for considering seriously the many questions I put to them and for being refreshingly open in explaining what they did and why. They have read the chapters about themselves but I am responsible if there are any errors in the facts or my interpretation.

In particular I must thank the following: at the Surrey Juvenile Resource Centre, John Dixon, the Team Manager, and Cath Harmes; at the Junction Project, Valerie Jones, the Project Leader, Julian Holder of Lambeth Social Services Department and Martin Farrell, formerly the Project Leader and now Secretary of the Institute for the Study and Treatment of Delinquency; in Kirklees, Mark Feeny, Principal Officer, Juvenile Justice, and Tony Homer, Barbara Martin and Moira Swann of the KEY projects; in West Sussex, John Platten, the former Project Leader, and his former colleagues John Gibson and Nicky Stenner (who reconvened on a Bank Holiday Saturday to meet me), Neil Morgan, Director of Chichester Diocesan Association for Family Social Work, Barry Anderson, now at NACRO but formerly of West Sussex Social Services Department, Dick Munnion of West Sussex Probation Service and Andrew Williamson, Deputy Director of Social Services, West Sussex County Council; in Berkshire, Richard Hayes, Principal Officer Children and Families, and Tom Butler, Service Development Officer, of Berkshire Department of Social Services; in Sunderland, Alan Dalton of Turning Point, Isabel Atkinson and other members of the Sunderland Youth Development Group, and Alan Jones, Principal Officer (IT), Borough of Sunderland.

I am also extremely grateful to many individuals for information, encouragement and helpful discussion but again I alone must take responsibility for the content of this book. I should like to thank especially Alison Skinner, Information Officer of the National Youth Bureau; Fran Gosling of NACRO; Judy Lister of the IT Fund; Archie Pagan, formerly of the DHSS; Ron Howell, formerly of the Rainer foundation and the IT Fund; Professor Norman Tutt and Dr Henri Giller of Social Information Systems; Professor Anthony Bottoms of Cambridge University Department of Criminology for allowing me to attend a seminar at which he presented some of the results of his current research; John Pitts of West London Institute of Higher Education; Christopher Hardy of West Sussex Institute of Higher Education; Richard Kay of the Rainer Foundation; Brian Johnson and Graham Sutton of the Home Office; Brian Hopper and Richard Duncombe of the DHSS and Chris Sealey of the DHSS Social Work Inspectorate; David Green, of HM Inspectorate, Department of Education and Science; Liz Thompson, Senior Chief Clerk, Inner London Juvenile Courts; my colleagues on the Inner London Juvenile Panel, the justices' clerks, the court staff, many who work in Intermediate Treatment, social work, educational social work and allied professions in Inner London; and the young people and families who appear in inner London juvenile courts, who have taught me much and made me want to write this book.

Finally, I want to thank my husband and our three sons for their constant support in all my undertakings.

London   S.C.
January 1989

1

The Patchwork Quilt of Provision

Intermediate Treatment is known, to the minority of people who realize that the initials IT do not stand for Information Technology, as a service for children and young people who are 'at risk or in trouble'. Although it is not mentioned by name in any Act of Parliament, young offenders are often referred to 'Intermediate Treatment projects' as a condition of Supervision Order made by a juvenile court. Yet to see Intermediate Treatment only as part of the criminal justice system would be to misunderstand its origins, its practice and its potential. Like the juvenile justice system in general, it has been bedevilled since its inception by overlapping and sometimes conflicting aims.

If you ask in different places what kind of young people attend Intermediate Treatment schemes, how old they are, how they were selected, what they do on them, how long they stay, whether they include girls as well as boys, whether their parents are involved, or whether they are all offenders, the answers you will receive will vary. The juvenile justice system has often been compared to a lottery, with the disposal received for an offence differing according to the locality, the temper of the region, or the facilities and services available to the Bench. The provision of Intermediate Treatment in England and Wales is like a patchwork quilt, with different areas offering different materials, some similar threads but often idiosyncratic stitching.

Pre-court diversion

In the past decade various screening procedures have been developed to divert young people from appearing in court. These include informal and formal cautioning by the police, scrutiny of the case by the local police

1

juvenile bureau, by a multi-agency panel, and by the Crown Prosecution Service which makes the decision of whether a case is brought to court. The CPS has to consider whether a prosecution is in the public interest as well as whether a case can be proved. Its guidelines state that it should refer back to the police any case against a juvenile where it considers that a lesser disposal, like a caution, would be an 'adequate response'.

These screening procedures have been encouraged because of evidence that once a young person has appeared in court, far from being deterred from crime, he or she is more likely to offend again.[1] On the other hand, cautions have been shown to be effective, with up to 80 per cent of those cautioned for the first time not coming to police notice again in the next two years.[2] Most important, there is a well-documented trend for young people to grow out of offending.[3] The peak age for male offending is 15 and the highest offending rate in the population is among male juveniles aged 14 and under 17, with seven per cent of this age-group cautioned or found guilty of an offence in 1986.[4]

However, the sifting mechanisms vary greatly in use and effectiveness according to the area.[5] A Home Office Circular in February 1985, *The Cautioning of Young Offenders*, sought to encourage a wider and more consistent use of cautioning. In 1986 two-thirds of juvenile offenders were cautioned but the variation in the use of cautioning between police forces was great: in Northamptonshire 81.75 per cent of the boys aged 14 to 16 who offended were cautioned, compared with 28.65 per cent in Staffordshire.

The multi-agency panels which exist in some areas include representatives from the police juvenile bureau, social services, and the education and youth services. Before a case is sent to the CPS they consider whether prosecution is necessary or whether the young person can be diverted from delinquency by voluntary supervision or arrangements, perhaps attendance at a youth club or at a local Intermediate Treatment centre without a court order. However, such panels are by no means established everywhere: in 1987, for example, the London Borough of Islington had one but not its neighbour Hackney which shares the same court premises.

The court process

What happens to those young people who have not been diverted from the courts but who have appeared in court and either admitted the offence or had the case against them proved? How does Intermediate Treatment fit among the disposals available to the court, a compulsory rather than a voluntary, preventive measures?

It is worth looking here at the terminology of the juvenile court. The word 'disposal' rather than 'sentence' is officially used for 'children' (boys and girls aged from ten to 13) and 'young people' (those aged 14 to 16). Until the rules were amended in 1988, juveniles were not asked in court whether they pleaded guilty or not guilty but whether they admitted or denied the charge. Such cumbersome phrases were difficult to understand – a good reason for changing them to the familiar words of court-room dramas – but they were intended to carry fewer overtones and indicate a distinction in attitude to juvenile offenders. Instead of saying 'You have been found guilty. This will be your punishment', the court was saying 'The case against you has been proved. This is what will happen as a result'. The wording was different on the pleas made (and still is about the disposals), to reflect the component in juvenile justice which, to a greater or lesser extent according to the priorities of the day, has looked to the welfare of young people since the separate juvenile court was established in 1908.

The element of welfare in disposals has not, however, been seen as beneficial by all. Apart from scepticism about the helpfulness of social work, there is still considerable argument about whether regard to the welfare of young people should entail interfering in their everyday lives in more depth or for longer than would be considered fair for adults. The 'justice' lobby puts forward the rights of the juvenile to receive the due process of the law, be punished for the offence and not be subjected to longer intervention. This tension between the right to justice and the need for welfare is a source of confusion for many working with young offenders.

Books about juvenile justice often give a list of disposals available to the court. A typical one was reproduced in the 1987 DHSS document *Reports to Courts. Practical Guidance for Social Workers*. It gave the following dispositions as available to the Court in criminal proceedings against juveniles in numbered order (but without the explanatory notes added here in square brackets):

1 Bind Over [A Bind Over is not in fact a disposal for an offence which has been admitted or proved but a separate order which may be made at the magistrates' discretion in addition to another disposal or, if the parties agree, when no case has been proved.]

2 Absolute Discharge
3 Conditional Discharge
4 Fine
5 Attendance Centre Order
6 Supervision Order [for up to three years] including [as well as conditions of residence]
   (a) Intermediate Treatment [the term is not used in the Act of Parliament but the guide to the Children and Young Persons Act 1969 refers to Intermediate Treatment as a requirement which may be added to a Supervision Order under Section 12(2) for up to 90 days. The activities are at the discretion of the supervisor.]
   (b) Stipulated or specified activity order [the activities are set down by the court, again for up to 90 days.]
   (c) Night Restriction Order
   (d) Refraining Order (from specified activities on specified days)
7 Care Order
8 Charge and Control Condition [on an existing Care Order made for an offence]
9 Community Service Order [for those over 16]
10 Detention Centre Order [for boys over 14]
11 Youth Custody [for those over 15]
12 Other Orders (Compensation, Hospital and Guardianship Orders, Parental Bind Over, Deferment, Ancillary Orders – Costs, Disqualifications, Endorsements).

Lists are useful for collating information but the way they are presented may influence the way they are interpreted. It is immediately apparent that the list reproduced here is not alphabetical. 'Absolute Discharge' may come first after 'Bind Over' but for reasons other than its alphabetical primacy. It is not followed by the next disposal beginning with 'a', the 'Attendance Centre Order', but by 'Conditional Discharge'. It is clear that this list, until the final miscellaneous grouping of 'Other Orders', is compiled on a supposed order of severity, beginning with the least punitive disposal.

Thus an Absolute Discharge denotes that an offence has been admitted or proved but that in the circumstances no further action is needed. A Conditional Discharge holds a sword of Damocles over the offender for a specified period: there is no punishment provided there is no new offence of any kind during this period but if the young person re-offends he or she is punished for the original as well as the new offence. In the parlance of juvenile court magistrates, the Conditional Discharge 'gives you a chance but doesn't let you off'. It is usually considered the least punitive disposal after the Absolute Discharge which is rarely used. Next come fines, often coupled on other lists with Compensation Orders, and then Attendance Centre Orders which send the young offender for a number of Saturday afternoons on a course, often run by police officers, of physical exercise and training in crafts or skills.

If the awards given by the state for outstanding service are a *cursus honorum*, this list of disposals might be termed the *cursus opprobriorum* for juveniles. In fact it is known as 'the tariff' and, despite much contrary evidence of disposals that are made out of tariff order, magistrates are often alleged to have the tariff at the front of their minds when making their decisions. For this reason social workers are sometimes advised when writing social inquiry reports for juvenile courts to canvass for the magistrates' consideration the 'lowest' penalty in the range in order to prevent the young person reaching custody at the top of the ladder too quickly. Although a first principle of sentencing is to select a disposal appropriate to the seriousness of the crime, it is thought that repeated offending makes magistrates reluctant to use disposals tried before or to use lesser penalties once more severe ones have been imposed.

In the list reproduced here and in most others, the Supervision Order would appear to be a middle-rank disposal. It comes after discharges, summary penalties like fines and the limited restriction of liberty through an Attendance Centre Order. The Supervision Order without conditions is flexible, leaving the number and timing of encounters between social worker and offender to the discretion of the supervising officer. However, the Order may include a requirement for the young person to participate for a maximum of 90 days in activities as directed by the supervisor. In addition, the Criminal Justice Act 1982 gave the juvenile court greater powers of direction, enabling it to order the young person to participate for a maximum of 90 days in specified activites as stipulated by the court. The term 'Intermediate Treatment' is not used in the Act and has no legal definition. What is commonly called an Intermediate Treatment Order is usually a Supervision Order with a requirement to participate for a set period in activities as instructed by the supervisor. A Supervision Order with a requirement to participate in specified activities as stipulated by the court is often referred to as a Specified Activities Order, although the activities are sometimes referred to in a general way as 'IT'.

The strengthened Supervision Order with activities specified by the court was introduced for the court to use when it wanted to ensure intensive work and probably speedier intervention than had been usual. In one of the few surveys of the conduct of Supervision Orders, Robert Harris and David Webb[6] found in 1978 that 24 per cent of those assigned for supervision to social services, and 12 per cent of those to probation, did not see their supervisors till seven weeks after the order was made. In the areas studied in this book, recommendations in social inquiry reports gave an immediate starting date for attendance at projects but a joint team of HM Inspectorate of Probation and the Social Services Inspectorate found in 1984–85[7] that 19.7 per cent of juveniles given Supervision Orders in two non-metropolitan counties were not seen within 30 days and 5.8 per cent were still waiting after 60 days, including some for whom Intermediate Treatment had been ordered.

At the end of such lists, whether they appear in textbooks for social workers or handbooks for magistrates, lie the orders which restrict the liberty of the offender by removing him or her from the community. Until 1988 there were two custodial orders, for Detention Centre and for Youth Custody (formerly a recommendation for Borstal training). The juvenile court could also commit a 15 or 16 year old to the Crown Court for sentence if it thought the length of custody it could impose was not sufficient for the offence. In 1988 the two custodial orders for juveniles were amalgamated into a single one of 'detention in a young offender institution'.

In addition, until the 1989 Children Act abolished them, Care Orders were still made in some criminal cases (1,000 in 1986) when the need for care or control had been proved as well as an offence. The number of Care Orders made in criminal cases had decreased because it was generally considered to be fairer to treat separately the needs of the child or young person for care or control. Offending may well be affected or precipitated by lack of parental care or control but the primary matter before the criminal court is the offence. An indeterminate order, made till the age of 18, giving the local authority immense power over the young person's life, might seem an unjust disposal for the offence and the young person's need for care or control better assessed by care proceedings.

The structure of such lists is logical in that custodial disposals are obviously the most severe penalties available. It is, however, simplistic and can be damaging to the interests of young people to think of the list as an immutable tariff and to imagine that courts choose disposals in a mechanical way. On the contrary, those who are making disposals are taught to begin from the nature and gravity of the offence. They then consider, and are especially mandated to do so for juveniles, the case of the individual offender. It will be seen in the course of this book that the alleged reluctance of magistrates to repeat disposals can be overcome by cogent reports offering good reasons. In addition, reliance on the theory of the tariff can be misleading as there are different perceptions of the gravity of certain disposals. The joint team of Probation and Social Services Inspectors found that social workers rated supervision as a comparatively severe disposal, likely to make offenders eligible for custody if they appeared in court again. Magistrates, however, tended to consider it as a supportive measure and disregarded any effect it might have on future disposals.

The road to custody was lengthened by the 1982 *Criminal Justice Act*, which permitted courts to make custodial orders on juveniles only if they were 'of the opinion that no other method of dealing with the defendant is appropriate because it appears to the court that (i) he is unwilling to respond to non-custodial penalties; or (ii) a custodial sentence is necessary for the protection of the public; or (iii) the offence is so serious that a non-custodial sentence cannot be justified'. The courts had in normal circumstances to obtain social inquiry reports to establish these facts and the defendant had to have legal representation. After evidence that these restrictions were not significantly reducing the number of custodial disposals and were not always being observed by magistrates,[8] they were clarified in 1988 to make it absolutely plain that custody for young people should be a last resort.

The DHSS and the Home Office

An outsider might expect schemes for Intermediate Treatment, attended as a disposal of the court under a Supervision Order, to be a Home Office responsibility, like the custodial institutions. The concept of Intermediate Treatment had indeed first been articulated in the Home Office document *Children in Trouble* which led to the Children and Young Persons Act 1969. The Civil Servant, Derek Morrell, who coined the logical name – the treatment lay between disposals which intervened little in the young person's life and those which disrupted it by removal from the community – was at the Home Office and it was the Home Office which at that time ran the nation's child care services. However, in 1971 local government welfare services were reorganized in the wake of the Seebohm Report. The child care services were incorporated in generic social services departments planned to meet the needs of everyone in the community without duplicating services. As a result, all services for children and young people came under the DHSS. The Home Office retained responsibility for all custodial provision, including that for juveniles, and for the probation service, which had the remit of carrying out work for the courts. In most areas, however, social services undertook the court work with children under 14 and probation with young people of 14 or older. The implications of different funding and responsibility for custodial and non-custodial disposals were important, as will be seen.

Through its work with children and young people the DHSS now had an involvement with the court process, while the Home Office retained a welfare role with some juveniles through the probation service. As has been indicated, it is often difficult to draw a line between punishment and welfare in penal matters. The duty of the probation officer who carries out a Supervision Order made by a court is 'to advise, assist and befriend' offenders but such attention can be seen as a restriction on their autonomy and an intrusion into their lives. Nevertheless, the practical help and moral support given by supervision are different from the punishment, retribution and reparation exacted by fines, custody, and community service.

Both approaches are put forward as deterrents of crime. From the 1960s evidence consolidated about the ineffectiveness of custody as a means of preventing young people from re-offending. Eighty-three per cent of those who finished Youth Custody Orders in 1983 were reconvicted within two years and 68 per cent of those who had served Detention Centre Orders. Statistics veil numerous factors. Were those sent to institutions 'infected' and taught new, smarter ways to offend by the other inmates? Did they now see themselves as criminals and like the cachet? Or had these young recidivists been deprived of their liberty too late to stop them in their tracks?

Some used the high failure rate of custody to argue for earlier punitive intervention, the short sharp shock of a short Detention Centre Order, which was then shown to be similarly ineffective in its results.[9] The moderate majority, however, pointed out the futility of sending young people away and then returning them to the community without any new equipment to deal with old problems. Those who saw juvenile delin-quents as partly the victims of their circumstances, poor housing, poor education, poor leisure facilities, poor employment prospects, few choices in life, were joined by the pragmatists who sought some other way to turn the young from crime since custody did not. It was a Conservative Government on a law and order mandate which agreed through its 1982 Criminal Justice Act that custody for young offenders should be a last resort 'where other measures were clearly inappropriate'.

The opportunity was there for Intermediate Treatment, used previously as a middle-rank penal disposal, to become a genuine alternative to custody. This change was supported on the one hand by those who believed the public had a right to know young thieves, vandals and robbers were punished, since Intermediate Treatment as an alternative to custody was to be no soft option. On the other hand, it was approved by those who saw Intermediate Treatment as the best way to help the personal development of the young person and to integrate him or her into conventional society. The question that was difficult, has taken years to formulate and in general is still unresolved, was whether Intermediate Treatment could be both an alternative to custody in the criminal justice system and a preventive measure to divert young people from ever crossing the threshold of a court. Could everyone involved, from the social workers, to the magistrates, to the teachers, to the parents, to the young people themselves, let alone the general public, grasp the distinction between what in many places became known as 'voluntary IT' and the Intermediate Treatment scheme which a young offender attended under a Supervision Order for up to 90 days, sometimes with specific activities set down, and with the sanction of a return to court for not attending?

The broad approach

The broad approach to two overlapping but distinct groups could be seen from the outset. The 1969 Children and Young Persons Act, which became law on 1 January 1971, enabled local authorities to set up schemes of community-based treatment for young offenders and other children at risk of appearing before the courts. The responsibility for planning and co-ordinating the schemes, integrating contributions from the statutory and voluntary sectors, was given to 12 Children's Regional Planning Committees. A 1977 circular from the DHSS (LAC(77)1) in its opaque way showed how wide the definition of Intermediate Treatment could be: 'Intermediate treatment facilities may also be provided as preventive measures for children not specifically "at risk" or in trouble but where a risk situation might result if the measures were not taken'. The obligation to set up schemes was not, however, backed by special finance. By 1976/77 the total amount spent by local authorities in England and Wales on Intermediate Treatment was only £1 for every £73 spent on residential care. In addition, they were preoccupied with the aftermath of local government and social services reorganization.

A survey in 1979 by the Youth Social Work Unit of the National Youth Bureau showed that at that time there were only 60 actual IT centres in England and Wales, more than half of which had opened in the previous two years. Intermediate Treatment schemes could of course operate without premises but the survey's definition of a centre was fairly open: 'A physical facility which provides a locale for work with young people by permanent staff who are based at the facility and at least one of whom is primarily engaged in what the project considers to be IT'.[10] Of the 47 centres which returned a questionnaire, 30 were established and/or managed by a local authority and 17 by non-statutory agencies. Just over a third had beds on the premises, since at that time most Intermediate Treatment programmes contained a residential element. The interesting point to note is that although well over half the statutory centres were working with young people on court orders after offending, the majority were intended as alternatives to residential care for children and young people whose families could not look after them and were focused on the general social and educational needs of disadvantaged young people.

There is no doubt that progress in building Intermediate Treatment nation-wide was slow in the first decade. In 1978 a new National Fund for Intermediate Treatment in England and Wales was set up by the then Secretary of State for Social Services. Although financed from government sources, the Fund was independently administered by the Rainer Foundation. It aimed to complement local authority initiatives in Intermediate Treatment by encouraging projects in the voluntary sector which were based in the community and whose existence would be welcomed by the statutory services. As the IT Fund, it today serves a similar, useful function. Its 1978 definition of Intermediate Treatment is worth quoting in full:

> Intermediate Treatment, within the context of community care, seeks to provide a wide range of educational, recreational and work-training opportunities designed to meet the identified needs of young people who are in trouble or at risk of being so. The purpose is to enable them to fulfil their potential and reach a standard of achievement which will give them the confidence to face the realities of the world they live in

and compete on equal terms with children from more secure backgrounds. This entails creating projects and opportunities where none exist, or modifying existing resources within the conventional social work and youth education system. Intermediate Treatment, therefore, stands between traditional social work methods, to which an increasing number of delinquents are failing to respond, and removal to institutional care which IT tries to avoid. But if the IT approach of attempting to solve a young person's problems whilst retaining him in the community is to be successful, it must be accepted by the community and involve caring members of the public in supporting community-based projects with their time and talents.

The statement goes on to give examples of types of activity offered to fulfil these ends, including remedial education, outdoor pursuits, leisure centres, sports, motor-bike maintenance and riding, job-finding skills, arts, crafts, photography, communication skills, group work and counselling. Here are many of the elements associated now with Intermediate Treatment: the development of individual skills, compensation for what has been missed in the past, an emphasis on group activities as well as individual counselling, a multi-disciplinary approach involving social work, education and youth work. The disadvantages of residential care, isolated from the community, are seen as well as those of custody. Offending itself is not, at any rate in the statement, shown as a topic to be addressed separately. This is not surprising since offenders are seen in tandem with those at risk. Most important, Intermediate Treatment is firmly placed in a continuum of services in the community for young people.

In its first annual report, dated June 1979, the Fund noted that an important fact to remember about delinquency was that the majority of young offenders grew out of it spontaneously and became law-abiding adults. It is probably this fact, combined with the high cost[11] and ineffectiveness of custodial measures, rather than belief in the general principle of treatment not punishment for young offenders, which has led to the widespread acceptance, a decade later, of the principle of diverting juveniles from the courts. The notion of treatment, thinking of delinquency in pathological terms as a disease to be cured on the medical model, is out of fashion. There is disquiet at a time of high unemployment among unqualified young people about the circumstances and prospects of teenagers but reluctance to say they cannot make moral choices. Hence many Intermediate Treatment projects retain an emphasis on improving practical skills but have increased their attempts to help individuals choose behaviour which is socially acceptable.

The endeavours of local authorities to provide a broad, preventive service as well as an alternative for custody for known offenders are shown in the preliminary findings of the major research project by Professor Anthony Bottoms and his associates at the Cambridge University Department of Criminology. The first stage of this DHSS-funded research was a national survey of Intermediate Treatment provision, the fieldwork for which was carried out in 1985.[12] The second phase is a detailed evaluation of Intermediate Treatment in four local authority areas (Doncaster, Hertfordshire, Leeds and Rotherham). The fieldwork for the second phase began in September 1987 and it is expected that the results will be published in 1990.

On the basis of the interviews they conducted in the first phase, the Cambridge team constructed a typology of the philosophy of Intermediate Treatment in different social services departments. They identified five categories: 'prevention pure' (no serious links with the juvenile justice system), 'prevention plus' (more interest in the juvenile justice system), 'alternatives to custody and care pure' (exclusively for those at serious risk of custody or care, with preventive work in their areas for non-offenders or lesser offenders not called Intermediate Treatment), 'alternatives to custody and care plus' (including some medium-range offenders) and 'broad-based' (comprising at least two key elements, targeted provision for the 'heavy-end' offenders and preventive work with non-offenders). The largest single category (chosen by 35 per cent of the respondents) was broad-based Intermediate Treatment. Sometimes it was developed as a planned strategy and sometimes it evolved on an *ad hoc* basis.

Alternatives to custody and care

The emergence of a form of Intermediate Treatment carefully aimed at those seriously at risk of being removed from home, whether for offending or through the breakdown of their families, can be seen in the recommendations of the report *A Future for Intermediate Treatment* produced by a study group of the Personal Social Services Council (PSSC) in 1977. The study group was chaired by Dr Mia Kellmer Pringle, the psychologist who, as Director of the National Children's Bureau, did much to focus the attention of the public as well as those in the child care professions on the needs of children. Its membership brought together the Director of NACRO (National Association for the Care and Resettlement of Offenders), who was at that time Nicholas Hinton, a former Chairman of the Juvenile Courts Committee of the Magistrates' Association (Lady James of Rusholme), Dr Norman Tutt, who became Professor of Applied Social Studies at the University of Lancaster but who was then Principal Social Work Service Officer at the DHSS, a Director of Social Services (Denis Allen), an HMI (Inspector) from the Education Service and one from the Home Office, and individuals working in Intermediate Treatment, residential care and the voluntary sector.

This talented group from different disciplines had been given the brief 'To examine the concept of Intermediate Treatment, in terms of its history and underlying philosophy, to consider how this is reflected in the relevant provisions of the Children and Young Persons Act 1969, and to clarify the nature and objectives of this form of treatment'. They initially defined Intermediate Treatment as 'Action through a range of community-based programmes planned to meet identified needs of children and young persons who are at risk of appearing or who have appeared before the courts'. The report points out that one of the tenets of *Children in Trouble* was that there should not be 'segregated groups composed wholly of delinquents'. The prime objective of non-residential treatment was for the young offender to receive the training he or she required in the community, and there would be risk of 'contamination' (as in institutions), if those in trouble were restricted to all-delinquent treatment groups. The PSSC group, however, proposed on an experimental basis an 'intensive' form of intermediate treatment for the persistently delinquent, in addition to other forms of Intermediate Treatment for which 'there should be no arbitrary limitation on participation'.

It hoped this new, intensive Intermediate Treatment would diminish the use of detention centres and Borstals for 15–17 year-olds and lead to more effective use of residential care for the few young people who needed it. The form the group envisaged the intensive Intermediate Treatment would take, included an initial residential placement of about two weeks, followed by an intensive daily programme, with opportunities for further short-term residential placements if appropriate. The initial residential component was seen partly as a period of assessment during which the later programme would be planned. Work experience was suggested for the programme as well as personal and social education. Perhaps more important than the details of the intensive

Intermediate Treatment proposed was the emphasis on making the objectives of the intervention clear to all concerned and on gaining the confidence of the magistracy. The idea of a multi-disciplinary team was applauded – 'Social workers, youth workers, probation officers, teachers and education welfare officers all have skills and different methods of work which will be of value in running a programme of this kind' – and the use of an external consultant for training staff was mooted.

The DHSS 1983 initiative

A decisive step in establishing Intermediate Treatment as an acceptable alternative to custody, and in making it more available, was taken in 1983 by the DHSS. A circular, LAC(83)3, issued on 26 January of that year, set out plans for the development of Intermediate Treatment which were to shape for the future this aspect of it. The initiative was remarkable for the way it set clear goals for a defined group of young people, encouraged partnership between statutory and voluntary agencies, advocated co-operation at management level between those working in the juvenile justice system, and tried to ensure that the new schemes would become permanent parts of the overall strategy of local authorities for the young in their areas. It did not, however, resolve the underlying confusion between Intermediate Treatment as an alternative for serious offenders and as a preventive measure for those at risk.

The carrot to encourage local authorities to back voluntary agencies in creating new projects was financial. In 1981/82 local authorities had spent an estimated £10m on Intermediate Treatment. Central Government had made £700,000 available to voluntary organizations and given £450,000 to the IT Fund to disburse. From April 1983 a further £15m was offered 'to help the development of more intensive Intermediate Treatment programmes, designed specifically for those young people who would otherwise go to Borstal or detention centres'. It was explained that although progress in opening facilities had been made, the use by the courts of custodial disposals for young people who had offended more seriously or persistently had not declined as much as had been hoped: 'no doubt because of the very patchy development of those intensive programmes of Intermediate Treatment specially intended as community-based alternatives'. The reason for the patchy development was tentatively ascribed to either caution among local authorities about committing substantial resources to what some would see as experimental work or as a transitional problem in releasing the necessary resources.

The grants were available to voluntary bodies sponsored by a local authority especially to provide additional intensive Intermediate Treatment facilities for inclusion in the local authority's Intermediate Treatment scheme for the area. The Criminal Justice Act 1982 had transferred, from the 12 Children's Regional Planning Committees, which were being wound down, to the local authorities the duty of making Intermediate Treatment provision. There were limits to the number of projects sponsored in each area in order to encourage as wide a take-up of the offer as possible. Full funding was initially planned for two years only and the local authority would be expected to say what their plans were for the funding of the facility after the grant-aid from the DHSS expired. The expectation of building a permanent resource was therefore clear from the outset. This was an example of pump-priming on set conditions.

Why was a partnership stipulated in the first place, between a voluntary body and the local authority? If the eventual aim was the incorporation of the project into the permanent resources of the area, why was the money not offered directly to social services departments to expand their provision? A cynic might say that the Government was aiming to cut costs in financing alternatives for young offenders, and there was certainly a desire to draw additional money from the community. However, the strategy also recognized that a voluntary organization was in a better position than a statutory agency to work quickly and to innovate. Voluntary organizations, from the Rainer Foundation to the big children's charities like Barnardo's, the Children's Society and Save the Children Fund, had been pioneers in running schemes in the community for young offenders and those at risk. They often had more experience of work in this field than social services departments.

The circular was sent not just to Directors of Social Services but to Chief Education Officers, the Crown Courts, Justices' Clerks, Magistrates, Chief Officers of police, the Probation Service and selected voluntary organizations. This distribution reflected the kind of management structure advocated in the guidelines for those applying for funds. The credibility of Intermediate Treatment as an alternative to custody depended on all those working in the system understanding its aims, knowing about the facilities being offered and backing them. If magistrates, the clerks of juvenile courts, police and teachers were on the management bodies on the new ventures, they would have a stake in their success and also a say in the way they developed.

The responsibility of monitoring the initiative was given to NACRO (the National Association for the Care and Resettlement of Offenders). The factors affecting the outcome of court disposals are so many and various that there is a dearth of reliable information about their effectiveness. We know that about 80 per cent of young people sentenced to custody re-offend within two years but there is no overall, systematic recording of rates of recidivism. The problem is aggravated by the cut-offs at 17 between the juvenile courts and the adult courts. One of the barriers Intermediate Treatment, as an alternative to custody, had to break was the suspicion that it did not deter grave or persistent offenders. Few would expect a 100 per cent success rate and it could be said that it would not be hard to better a rate whereby four-fifths of those young people who had been in custody or detention were again caught in the act within a couple of years. However, until the 1983 initiative there had been no attempt to collate the outcome of Intermediate Treatment at a national level.

The concept of assessing outcome in terms of preventing reoffending was itself suspect for some. Did it not narrow the potential of Intermediate Treatment in developing young people as individuals, concentrating on one aspect of their behaviour which should better be seen in the context of the whole of their progress to maturity? The specific remit of the 1983 initiative to provide intensive facilities for those who were known as the 'heavy-end' offenders, those on statutory 90-day programmes ordered by the courts, focused attention on the need to convince courts and the public that juvenile crime was being prevented.

A total of 110 projects providing alternatives to Custody and Care Orders were established through the 1983 initiative in 62 of the 116 local authority areas in England and Wales. A six-month extension grant was given to some but many were ending their initial phase by the time the last, the Boathouse Project in the Pimlico area of the City of Westminster, opened its doors in May 1987. The results of the fourth census of projects conducted by NACRO were published in December 1987. Four of the projects were unable to contribute to the survey because they had closed, and 11 had opened after the beginning of the census period.

It is a pity that only 65 of the remaining 95 projects completed replies, despite the emphasis on monitoring their work, placed in the original terms on which they were given grants. The response rate for each question from those who did reply was also unsatisfactory, ranging from 68 per cent to only 33 per cent on one question. The NACRO note on the response rate comments that many project monitoring systems are still 'in the developmental stage'. The weakness of monitoring systems throughout the juvenile justice system means that there is a dearth of relevant facts on which to make decisions. The arguments for devoting money to monitoring are cogent.

On the available information, however, the report was able to posit for the first time the effect of the new Intermediate Treatment schemes as a factor in reducing the number of 14 to 16 year-olds sent into custody. From the survey of 65 projects in 42 local authority areas, it was shown that in the last six months of 1986 half the number received custodial sentences as had in the same period in 1985. The reduction in the number of Care Orders was even bigger: they fell from 112 to 36. The national statistics on custodial disposals for 1986 also showed falls. The number of custodial orders fell to 4,400 from 6,000 in 1985 and a peak of 7,700 in 1981: as a proportion of those sentenced or cautioned the use fell from 6 per cent in 1985 to 5 per cent, but the main reduction was at detention centres (from 4,000 orders in 1985 to 2,900 in 1986) rather than in youth custody (2,000 orders fell to 1,500).

The climate of opinion changes all the time and doubtless magistrates were to some extent reflecting, in the orders they made, the unease in the social work profession and the general public about removing young people from home except when essential. To compare the treatment of children in local authority care, in 1976 only a third of children in public care were fostered in families. The rest were in children's homes or other institutions. As the benefits were stressed of individual attention and family life for children whose own parents could not look after them, so more foster parents were recruited to care for them, not in an open-ended way but to complete a specific task for an agreed time. Some were trained to give stability to difficult teenagers, receiving a fee as 'professional' foster parents in addition to the usual boarding-out allowance which only covers what the child costs the family. More were trained to cope sympathetically with the child's own family and, as appropriate, to help in rehabilitating the child at home or finding new, adoptive parents. By 1987 the proportion of children in care who were fostered had increased to half. Professional and public awareness had effected a shift of resources from residential to community care, enabling more foster parents to be recruited and trained, and therefore more children to be placed with foster parents rather than in children's homes.

In a similar way it was only possible for magistrates to order Intermediate Treatment in place of custody if there were suitable facilities in their area. By making new money available to establish intensive Intermediate Treatment schemes, the Government increased the choices open to the juvenile court. The report on the fourth census of projects set up under the 1983 initiative stated that 'though there are some regional variations in sentencing, these are very much less pronounced in areas with Intermediate Treatment projects than elsewhere.'

On the other hand, the report showed that custody was still being used for non-violent offenders and those with few, if any, previous convictions. The popular image of the young person in custody is of a thug who beat up an old lady for her savings. In fact, only 16 per cent of those in the survey given Custodial or Care Orders had committed offences of violence, sex or robbery. Violence was a factor in only 7 per cent of offences by juveniles in 1986. The thug in custody is often presumed to be a hardened offender. In this survey one-fifth of those given custody had no previous convictions and almost one half had only two or fewer. It would follow from the Criminal Justice Act 1982, that their crimes must have been extremely serious to bring custody upon them or necessitate the protection of the public by their detention, since these were the conditions to be fulfilled under the Act before a custodial disposal might be imposed on a young person, unless he or she had proved unwilling to respond to other measures. It emerges that the definition of seriousness and the assessment of when the public needs protection vary as much from area to area as the provision of facilities. On average, almost half the orders for custody or care made on males aged between 14 and 16 in the census period of the survey were made after burglaries. However, in the DHSS North Region two-thirds were made after burglaries, compared with fewer than one-third in London and the South East.

One question asked by the census concerned the ethnic origins of those attending the projects. This was the question with the least number of replies, reflecting the reluctance in the juvenile justice system to collect data about race, despite the arguments that such information is needed. It has been suggested that black young people are over-represented in all aspects of the juvenile justice process, from the number picked up by the police, to the number brought to court rather than cautioned, to the number given custodial rather than other disposals for less serious offences and with fewer previous convictions.[13] From the 28 projects which were able to give details about the racial origins of young people receiving Custody or Care Orders, it emerged that 8 per cent were black but that only 5 per cent of those on project programmes were black.

The report concluded that the increased numbers of offenders attending projects were genuinely those who would previously have attracted a custodial disposal. Despite this success, and despite preliminary indications that the final verdict on the 1983 initiative will be that it also set welcome standards of inter-agency and interprofessional co-operation, the Government had no plans in 1988 to repeat the venture.

Clarifying goals

The extensive survey by Professor Bottoms and his Cambridge team will, within a few years, produce detailed information about the nature and content of Intermediate Treatment at the time of their research. In addition, the DHSS in 1988 planned an official inspection of Intermediate Treatment in at least three regions by its Social Services Inspectorate, with Her Majesty's Inspectors of Schools also involved. It was expected to focus on the place of Intermediate Treatment within the agency's overall child care policy, the organizational arrangements for its delivery, its effectiveness and its costs.

In this book examples are given from six areas of projects practising what might be described as Intermediate Treatment, even if that is not the label used by the projects. To some extent the choice of projects was arbitrary, although care was taken to describe northern as well as southern ventures, one with a rural catchment area as well as urban projects, and to look at preventive work in two areas as well as several examples of projects which were alternatives to custody. The aim is not to give a comprehensive overview of Intermediate Treatment but to show from these few examples how many approaches to the task are possible. There are crucial differences in the way these projects began, are managed, are organized from day to day, between the staff they have, their relationships with other agencies, the role they see for themselves, how they fit into the general strategy for youth in the area (when there is such a strategy), and how they work with young people and their families. These differences must be understood if the goals of what we now call Intermediate Treatment are to be clarified for the future.

The recent increase in the number of Intermediate Treatment projects has uncovered a need for practical examples of work for which there are no specific qualifications and few national training courses. Those who entered work in Intermediate Treatment as social workers may have qualified as social workers after the present two-year course with minimal theoretical or practical instruction in child development,[14] the law concerning children and young people, or delinquency. The main focus for those who trained as teachers will have been their academic subjects and teaching techniques; nor will delinquency have been the central concern for youth and community workers. The only post-qualifying course on work with young offenders considered for approval by CCETSW (the Central Council for Education and Training in Social Work) in 1988 was that run by the West Sussex Institute of Higher Education at Bognor Regis. Nearly all training is acquired after appointment, on the job or through in-service courses often arranged by local branches of the National Intermediate Treatment Federation (NITFed).

The projects are reported as their staff presented them. Examples are given of the methods they use, the reports and letters they write, their publicity material for the different people with whom they work, and their use of monitoring. The views of their staff are given about their aims and plans. The voices of the young people who attend the projects are only heard indirectly through progress sheets, or sometimes through material they have produced at the projects. It is unfortunate that there are at present very few[15] reports from consumers about their experiences of Intermediate Treatment, but the only way to obtain useful responses from young people is to spend a great deal of time with them, a research project in itself.

References

1 MORRIS, A., and GILLER, H., *Understanding Juvenile Justice*, Croom Helm, 1987.
RUTHERFORD, A., *Growing out of Crime*, Penguin, 1986.
WEST, D., *Delinquency. Its roots, Careers and Prospects*, Heinemann, 1982.
2 *Time for Change. A New Framework for Dealing with Juvenile Crime and Offenders*, NACRO, 1987, p. 15.
3 Rutherford, op. cit.
4 *Criminal Statistics, England and Wales, 1986*, Cmnd 233, HMSO, 1987.
5 RICHARDSON, N., *Justice by Geography?*, Social Information Systems, 1987.
6 HARRIS, R., and WEBB, D., *Welfare, Power and Juvenile Justice*, Tavistock, 1987.

7 HM INSPECTORATE OF PROBATION; HOME OFFICE AND SOCIAL SERVICES INSPECTORATE, *Report on the Practice of Supervision of Juvenile Offenders*, DHSS, 1987.

8 BURNEY, E. 'All things to all men: justifying custody under the 1982 Act', *Criminal Law Review*, 1985, pp. 284–90; *Sentencing Young People*, Gower, 1985.

9 *Tougher Regimes in Detention Centres*, Report of an evaluation by the Young Offender Psychology Unit, Home Office, HMSO, 1984.

10 LOCKE, T., *Intermediate Treatment Centres*, Youth Social Work Unit, National Youth Bureau, 1980.

11 In 1986–87 the cost of youth custody in a closed establishment was £278 a week, and the cost in an open establishment £332 a week for males, £343 a week for females.

12 BOTTOMS, A., 'Cambridge Research into Intermediate Treatment', *Youth Social Work*, 5 November 1987, pp. 20–23.

13 BERRY, S., *Ethnic Minorities and the Juvenile Court*, Nottingham Social Services Department, 1984.

LANDAU, S., and NATHAN, G., 'Selecting delinquents for cautioning in the London Metropolitan area', *British Journal of Criminology*, April 1983.

MARTIN, D., *Afro-Caribbean Clients in Youth Custody*, South-east London Probation Service, 1985.

Race and Justice for Young Offenders, NACRO Briefing, 1987.

SMITH, D., *Police and People in London*, Policy Studies Institute, 1983.

STEVENS, P., and WILLIS, C. F., *Race, Crime and Arrests*, Home Office Research Study No. 58, HMSO, 1979.

14 DREWRY, G., ed., *After Beckford? Essays on Themes Related to Child Abuse*, Department of Social Policy, Royal Holloway and Bedford New College, 1987.

15 See, however, young people's comments in IXER, G., 'The experience of tracking', in *In Search of Another Way: Working with Young Offenders*, A Voice for the Child in Care and The Children's Society, 1987, and JONES, R., *Like Distant Relatives*, Gower, 1987.

2

Ending Custody
The Juvenile Offender Resource Centre, Surrey

The Surrey Juvenile Offender Resource Centre is clear about its aims and confident about the contribution it makes to services for young people in Surrey. It exists first and foremost 'to reduce, wherever possible, the number of young people in Surrey receiving Care Orders or custodial sentences for offending'. Its name shows the focus of its concerns and their span. It is not only a centre for providing activities as specified by the 11 juvenile courts in the county. In addition, it has 16 year-olds on Community Service Orders and runs pre-employment and accommodation schemes in which young people participate on a voluntary basis. Although it also aims to improve the quality of life for the young people who attend, it makes it plain, even in its title, that they are there in the first place compulsorily, as a punishment for the offences they have committed. It takes only young people who are in immediate danger of custody, and in its first years has helped to effect a reduction in the number of orders for custody and care from 16 per cent of all disposals for juveniles in Surrey in 1982, to 2.5 per cent in 1987.

The proportion of young people in the population is declining at the moment in the UK, an important factor to consider when analysing statistics about offending. Surrey has a slightly smaller proportion than average of young people aged under 18 in its population, 22.6 per cent, compared with 23.6 per cent in England and Wales as a whole. It also records the lowest offending rate in England and Wales for male juveniles aged between 14 and 17, only 2.2 per cent, compared with the national rate for 1986 of 7 per cent for this age-group. Leafy Surrey with its prosperous towns and villages cannot be described as a den of iniquity, even if it is a mistake to think that all its citizens enjoy adequate incomes and lead blameless lives. It may have a less serious crime-rate than some inner city areas but the offenders attending the Centre include boys with more than one offence of violence. In addition, courts in the shires often take a graver view of crimes against property than metropolitan ones. Surrey's use of Custody and Care Orders in 1982 for 14 to 16 year-old males was above the national average, but by the end of 1986 it was the lowest of 12 recorded by Social Information Systems, the monitoring and consultancy service on juvenile justice systems directed by Dr Henri Giller. The overall percentage of male offenders in England and Wales aged between 14 and 16 given Custody or Care Orders in 1986 was 14 per cent.

What elements in its structure have contributed to the Centre's success in diverting hard core offenders from custody? There is no doubt that its clarity of purpose as part of a strategy for young offenders developed by Surrey since 1983 has been crucial. Before that time there were virtually 11 separate juvenile justice systems attached to the 11 juvenile courts in the county, resources were scarce and scattered and there was little co-operation between the different agencies dealing with young people. The result was that young people received different treatment depending on where they lived and there was no unified information system to monitor what was happening. This haphazard situation was typical of juvenile justice in many areas.

The change came in 1983 when the Probation and Social Services Departments decided to work together in a single county-wide strategy and grasped the opportunity offered by the DHSS IT initiative in Circular LAC(83)3 to expand. The Centre was originally set up in 1983 to provide a supervised activities scheme for court orders. From the outset it had some success, reducing custodial sentences in Surrey in its first full year by over 20 per cent. In 1984 its range was extended when Surrey Probation Service decided to locate its new Community Service Scheme for 16 year-olds at the Centre, separate from its scheme for adults. This separate siting of a community service scheme for 16 year-olds, putting the emphasis on their age, is and was unusual, if not unique. Instead of the arrangements for the work and any subsequent interviews being conducted in the ordinary probation headquarters, the officers concerned operated from the place where there were other resources for juveniles and colleagues who concentrated on this age-group.

The final transformation was effected through the DHSS IT initiative. One of the features of the DHSS initiative was its requirement for interagency co-operation. Surrey had already begun this through the partnership between Probation and Social Services. However, money under the initiative was available only to new projects administered by a voluntary organization supported by statutory agencies. Surrey was again fortunate (or prescient) in having in existence the Surrey Care Trust, created by the Probation Service and the Probation Committee of Magistrates. Magistrates were another key group whose involvement was required by the DHSS initiative. As they were already involved, it was necessary only for the Surrey Care Trust Board to broaden its representation to include the police, social services, youth work, and clerks to the justices. It could then apply for funding under the initiative for a countywide scheme based on the existing Centre with resources used to choose staff capable of creating programmes for juveniles up to the age of 17, which were convincing alternatives to custodial punishment or institutional care.

The new scheme was officially launched on 1 February 1985. The staff appointed reflected the inter-agency structure of the management, with no more than two workers coming from the same professional background. At the beginning two came from probation, two from teaching, two from residential social work, one was a field social worker, one a youth worker and one had child care experience. The main roles of the Centre were to provide:

(a) facilities to Surrey courts for sentences which were alternatives to care or custody, including the preparation of assessment reports for the courts as well as the operation of the programmes;
(b) a consultancy service for social workers and probation officers preparing court reports on juveniles;
(c) specialist resources for professionals involved with young people or families, whether through help with staff, budgeting or equipment.

The Centre offered the courts three types of programme as alternatives to custody or care through a shared system of referral so that the most suitable plan could be offered for each individual. The three programmes were:

(a) community service for 16 year-olds, defined as 'disciplined, supervised work by way of reparation for young people of 16 years';
(b) a supervised activity scheme, defined as 'a Centre-based group programme of confrontation, reparation and rehabilitation for 14–16 year-olds';

(c) an intensive community programme, defined as 'intensive individual programmes tailored to the needs of young offenders aged 14–16 years, based in their own localities'.

It was clear from the beginning that the Centre would not operate in isolation. It was not merely to be a place to which young people were sent to be processed, but it had a crucial role in shaping the response to offending. The various people and components in the juvenile justice system were seen as connected, the actions of each affecting others. Thus, social workers and probation officers writing reports to the courts had to know the spectrum of penalties and intervention available for young offenders at every stage. They had to understand the nature of the alternatives the Centre offered to custody or care and the Centre's assessment process to choose the right programme for each boy or girl. When the Centre presented its assessment to the courts it was vital that the magistrates understood exactly what each programme entailed and why it was proposed in each case. The quality of the work done with the offenders at the Centre would obviously be crucial but what happened before and after referral was essential to its success.

Reports and programmes

The simplest way to show how the Centre operates is to look at some reports to the courts offering programmes for young people who have offended seriously and persistently. Although names and some details have been changed to prevent any young person being identified, reports are otherwise reproduced verbatim, both here and elsewhere in this book.

The first example is of a 16 year-old boy – let us call him Jim – before the court for having committed Grievous Bodily Harm and Threatening Behaviour. Grievous Bodily Harm is an offence of violence which would certainly satisfy the criterion of seriousness laid down as necessary to justify custody in the Criminal Justice Act, even as amended in 1988. He had assaulted a policeman, and at the time of the hearing it was not known whether the policeman would lose the sight of one eye. In addition, it emerges straightaway that Jim has enjoyed plenty of help in the community already. He has already been on two 'alternative to custody' programmes so it could be argued under the Act that he had failed to respond to the alternatives in the community offered to him. We see below how the officer from the Juvenile Offender Resource Centre argued and convinced the court that this boy should be given a 90-day intensive community programme requirement as a condition of a Supervision Order under Section 12(3)c of the Children and Young Persons Act 1969. The seriousness of Jim's position is indicated by the length of the order requested. The Centre rarely proposes programmes lasting as long as 90 days. The court in question was the Crown Court, where the case had been sent by the magistrates who felt that their powers to deal with it might not be sufficient. The Crown Court in question had no previous knowledge of the Centre.

The report, marked Confidential, is on the Juvenile Offender Resource Centre's headed paper, with the name and address of the officer writing the report at the top, followed by details of the boy, the court, his age, date of birth, occupation (unemployed), and the charge. The report then reads:

1   In presenting this report I am aware that it is unusual to request consideration for a third alternative to custody programme. In this case, too, the offences for which Jim has been found guilty are most unpleasant as well as serious. I understand that the time may well have come when there appears to be no other alternative to incarceration. However, it is under these circumstances and for reasons outlined below that I am nevertheless presenting a 90-day Intensive Community Programme.

2   Unless the relationship between Jim's anti-social behaviour and family difficulties (already identified and monitored) is tackled without further delay and directly alongside the root causes of his offending behaviour then I can see no alternative for this lad in the long term other than a continual repetition and escalation of offending with periods of incarceration interspersed with periods of hardening anger, bitterness, frustration and perhaps increasing aggression.

3   Jim has been visited at the remand centre where he is at present on three occasions in order to assess whether he is able and willing to be considered for an Intensive Community Programme. He recognizes the local community's demand for punishment and his own position with regard to his past offending history. He acknowledges, therefore, the purpose and severity of a 90-day programme and the social, emotional and physical demands that such a structure, discipline and punishment would impose on him.

Response to Previous Court Order

4   Fourteen months ago the Juvenile Court ordered Jim to attend the Juvenile Offender Resource Centre for a 45-day Supervised Activity Requirement. He had already received a Detention Centre sentence six months before and it was clear that this sentence had not addressed the source or effects of his offending behaviour.

5   The Supervised Activity Requirement was completed in nine months (six months ago) during which time Jim had been co-operative but diffident towards a group orientated programme. It became clear that 'sufficient progress took place whilst subject to a scheme alternative to custody, to warrant consideration of a further alternative' and that further work was possible with both Jim and his family which has 'potential for affecting attitudes and responsibilities'. (Quoted from the final Supervised Activity Report by his Juvenile Offender Resource Centre officer to his probation officer.)

6   Towards the end of this order Jim did re-offend. Unfortunately, the Court Order [he then received] for 100 hours of Community Service was unable to provide the intensive individual counselling that was needed a few months later. A Community Service Order, whilst providing in Jim's case extremely punitive indirect reparation (see progress report by the Community Service officer attached), does not include support from the Juvenile Offender Resource Centre other than Sunday supervision. Nevertheless, Jim was seeking help from both his probation officer and the Juvenile Offender Resource Centre at this stage. He made efforts to ween himself away from solvent abuse and visited the Solvent Abuse Clinic. Prior to this, he had obtained employment on a pig farm and had been trying to avoid getting into trouble. However, the improving situation could not develop further whilst Jim remained unable to ask his family for support.

Proposed Intensive Community Programme

7   By the time of this court appearance Jim will have spent six weeks in custody. During this time the options available in the creation of this programme have increased and it is for this reason that I am offering a different programme to the one available to the juvenile court recently.

8 The proposed 90-day Programme contains the following components:

(a) The first impact of the Intensive Community Programme will be to remove Jim from the home and immediate community. It will be clear from other reports available to the Court that substantial intervention is needed in the home environment. Jim, too, recognizes the importance of this intervention and has volunteered to complete the first three weeks of this sentence in North Wales. This means that 89 days of the programme will be put into effect after his return from a physically strenuous and mentally exacting Outward Bound Course. Jim has admitted that he finds this one of the most daunting aspects of the proposed sentence.

(b) *Community service* The nature and intensity of this punitive reparation is deliberately emphasized within the construction of the programme. Thus Jim will complete 31 days of Saturday and Sunday community work offering disciplined and supervised work to the disadvantaged, the handicapped and the elderly within his immediate locality. [This did not mean 31 full days but the equivalent of a Community Service Order of 120 hours often comprising two or three hours a day, in the mornings or afternoons.] For the first three weeks of the programme, Jim will spend an additional three days per week working for the Community (the other two days being spent in our Pre-Employment group detailed below). If Jim obtains full-time employment during this period, the remaining weekday Community Service on the schedule will be completed as weekend placements.

(c) *Weekend employment* Jim will attend our Pre-Employment group run by a qualified Youth Training Scheme instructor and a local ex-businessman in our workshops. Individual programmes of work experience, employable skills and social skills training are designed to lead into suitable full-time employment.

(d) *Individual sessions* The purpose of these sessions will be two-fold:

i) *Intervention into the home environment* Initially, Jim will be housed through our controlled accommodation scheme away from his home area. If this is to be an effective method of rehabilitation then work with the whole family will be necessary in order to promote either a movement into semi-independent living or eventual return home. Ten family meetings have been programmed for this purpose.

ii) *Individual Counselling* 33 sessions lasting until nine months from now. These will develop work that has already been done with regard to personal development, social and life skills therapy and to confront the root causes of Jim's anti-social behaviour. Close liaison will be maintained with the Probation Officer throughout in order to assist his supervision of Jim during the 10-month sentence.

(e) *Community placement* Supervised evening activities from Monday to Saturday inclusive chosen to promote constructive and purposeful use of leisure time. For example, helping at a local Physically Handicapped and Able Bodied club. The Saturday evening placement will be compulsory for the next four months.

Recommendation

9 The recommendation is for a 90-day Intensive Community Programme Requirement as a condition of a Supervision Order under Section 12(3)c of the Children and Young Persons Act 1969. A schedule of the proposed programme is attached to this report.

As well as the Centre's assessment report, the Court had the benefit, as indicated, of a social enquiry report by Jim's probation officer which described his complicated and unsatisfactory relationship with his family, his solvent abuse and previous criminal offences. The longest document, however, consisted of 5 pages giving the details of what he would do during the day and in the evening for the prescribed 90 days. Every single day is listed in the following manner:

Saturday 13 April	Daytime	Community Service
	Evening	Community Placement
Sunday 14 April	Daytime	Community Service
	Evening	Family Visit
Monday 15 April	Daytime	Pre-Employment Group
	Evening	Individual Sessions

The report has a number of striking features. It could be said to be emotive in its choice of words: 'incarceration', for example, is used for custody and a crescendo of phrases at the beginning gives a sense of crisis and impending doom for Jim. Yet the main impression is made through the details of the disposals already meted out to Jim and the reasons why they were not effective in stopping his offending. The conclusion the reader is led to, is that the causes of his behaviour are so deep-seated and complicated that it would be naïve to expect instant reform, a conclusion which in principle is sound concerning a great deal of offending by juveniles. The repetition of Supervision Orders with requirements for specified activities thus appears reasonable, a logical course of action for slow learners. After all, everyone knows that it takes months if not years for children to acquire cognitive skills like reading. The development of a moral sense is similarly a slow, cumulative process and behaviour is made habitual by practice.

The report seems to have been framed to anticipate a dialogue on these lines:

Court He's had everything the community can offer already. What's next on the tariff?

JORC The only way he will learn is through the same lesson being repeated.

Court Won't we be letting him off?

JORC No, it's a lesson he doesn't like and he has got to learn to accept lessons he doesn't like.

In fact an exchange in court between the judge and the officer from the Centre did follow similar lines, with the officer arguing that this time the programme had a different focus. The Centre did not say it could stop Jim from offending but that it could try to address the root causes of his behaviour in ways custody could not. Therefore it had a better chance than a custodial sentence of offering protection to the public in the long term.

Thus the second card the report plays is that although the vehicle is the same (the Section 12(3)c Order), the passengers in it and the route it takes each time are slightly different. The strength of the Centre shows here, first of all in its partnership with other agencies. The role of Jim's probation officer is key as counsellor and co-ordinator, and the Centre is able to combine types of disposal and approach. Jim will go on a residential course at the outset, to convince local people that something is happening as much as to stretch and shake up Jim, (local press reports of the case had shown the amount of feeling generated by the case among both the public and the police), and then do community service, undergo individual counselling and meetings with his family, learn skills in a pre-employment group, and live in a special accommodation scheme. Thus although the court is being asked to stick to the same vehicle, that vehicle is not being driven repeatedly up the same cul-de-sac.

The pre-employment and accommodation schemes

The scope of the Juvenile Offender Resource Centre has been widened under the Surrey Care Trust by the development of a pre-employment scheme and an accommodation scheme. Unemployment is an obvious hazard for young people at risk of offending. They are the least likely to win the jobs available as they usually have the fewest qualifications and poor school reports as well as their criminal records. If they have to leave home to seek work, there are no hostels for them to live in and they cannot afford rented accommodation even if they are mature enough to manage to live independently.

The JORC Pre-Employment Group is open to those who have left school, but lack the basic skills required both to find work and to maintain their commitment to a job. In Surrey in 1986 there were jobs available to young people with skills so the group could offer realistic goals and rewards. It had two part-time group leaders, one from an aeronautical engineering background, and the other with extensive experience of building and carpentry. They taught new skills, how to look for a job and interview techniques. They helped young people through the maze of their entitlements to benefit and above all, for three days a week they re-accustomed them to the routine of a working day.

Many participants were not only unemployed but had also been more often absent than present during their last year at school and it was too late for the Education Welfare Department to pursue them or their parents with orders to attend. The group had no official funding and used a large derelict greenhouse for premises. It had attracted support from industry and the community through publicity on local radio. Several thousand pounds' worth of industrial machinery had been donated, including two lathes, a band saw and a pattern cutting machine. Subsequently, the sessional worker with experience in building and carpentry was employed full-time through a grant from the national IT Fund. The Pre-Employment Group then built its own new workshop, a 'demountable' building constructed out of three condemned demountable buildings previously owned by the Education Department. By this means the County Council was saved £3,000 for demolition fees and given a building worth approximately £15,000.

The accommodation scheme is a radical venture. Instead of using, for example, professional foster parents, trained and given a fee and boarding-out allowance to act as surrogate parents to these difficult teenagers (who are often at odds with their families or whose parents cannot support them adequately in any way), the scheme recruits landlords and landladies on a commercial basis. Advertisements in the local press did not say 'Have you room in your home for a teenager who needs you?' but 'DO YOU NEED EXTRA CASH? Friendly lodgings required in Surrey for homeless young people. Long/short term. Rent guarantees given. For further details telephone . . .' (*County Border News* 18 September 1986).

The scheme is a joint initiative of the Social Services Department and the Probation Service, linking with borough housing departments, youth and community and housing associations. In the first year of its operation, from April 1986 to March 1987, it placed 83 young people from 251 who applied, many of whom would have been received into care without the scheme. The argument for looking for digs rather than surrogate parents is that the young people receive the support and counselling they need through their social workers, probation officers or the Centre. Their need for housing is separate and can be more effectively met separately. In their digs they are given a key to the front door and expected to obey the rules of the household, taking breakfast and the evening meal with the family. The scheme also negotiates with housing associations and the housing department to find permanent accommodation for young people.

In addition to the lodgings, the scheme now has a network of shared houses which offer accommodation for up to three young people living with a 'responsible adult'. A new inter-agency scheme has also been launched called Triple Key which provides a partnership between the accommodation scheme, the Royal Philanthropic Society and a special needs housing association.

Other persistent offenders

Was Jim's an exceptional case, asking for a third alternative to custody sentence for a 16 year-old who had assaulted and harmed a policeman? Certainly there are not many cases of violence in Surrey, but the kind of persistent offending which in some areas can inexorably lead to custody is more frequent. The JORC convinced the Crown Court in Jim's case that its programme was appropriately punitive and more likely than custody to stem Jim's offending. Another 16 year-old was before the juvenile court in 1987 for burglary, two offences of stealing and driving away motor vehicles (one an ambulance) and with other offences to be taken into consideration. A fourth alternative to the custody option was requested, and given, to Dave, as we shall call him.

Dave was in care, and for over three years had lived in a community home, while desperately wishing to return either to his mother, a single parent with five other children, or his father who had recently remarried. After a breakdown of his relationship with workers at the community home, he was remanded on bail to his mother. 'Ironically', says the JORC report 'by re-offending Dave had got what he had been aspiring towards for three and a half years: a return home'. But, 'owing to staff shortages' he was given no training for his new independence nor was his mother given help about managing him on his return. He rang the Centre saying he had a crisis and asking for help but then took the ambulance – 'I just did it – the keys were there' – to look for his girlfriend who had run away from home. He took a car a few weeks later, when he was asked to leave home late at night after an argument.

The Centre's request to the magistrates was for a new attempt at structured supervision, including community service at the weekends, community placements two evenings a week, art therapy at a specialist clinic and counselling to help him understand his anti-social behaviour, come to terms with his rejection by his family and manage independent living. The nub of the report was contained in the following paragraph:

> A custodial sentence will punish this juvenile by depriving him of his liberty. Whether its effect will be any longer-lasting than the 80 per cent reconviction rate for custodial disposals published by the Home Office suggests, will depend on whether the institutional environment is able to heal or harm further. A treatment-based programme such as the one recommended, is designed both to punish and to rehabilitate this young person into an adult socialized world in which he has got to learn how to live and work or alternatively to spend the majority of his life in and out of prison establishments.

As with Jim, the report spelt out in minute detail exactly what Dave would be doing and when. The JORC leaves nothing to chance, even offering the magistrates 'suggested wording' for the order. In Dave's case the suggested wording adopted was:

> And the defendant, having consented, shall comply with the following requirement:
> In pursuance of Section 12(3)c of the Children and Young Persons Act 1969 the defendant will participate in the following activities on 65 days.

1 He will take part in a programme of services to the Community on 17 days.

2 He will attend the Juvenile Offender Resource Centre or at a place specified by his worker on 23 occasions to undertake programmes designed to address offending and anti-social behaviour.

3 He will attend an approved Community Facility on 23 occasions.

4 He will attend as directed on 2 occasions specified by his supervising officer.

The magistrates were also given an example of the report sheet which would be completed for Dave after each session. This names the session, gives the time he was picked up and dropped off, and his response. The response is measured on a scale of five, monitoring punctuality, behaviour/conduct, response to supervisor, co-operation with group, quality of work and suitability of placement. There is space for comments and the form is signed by both the worker and by Dave. The continuing involvement of the young person in the assessment of his own progress is a feature of the JORC approach. The aim is to make the young person face the reality of what is happening and take responsibility for his or her own actions.

Jason is an example of a younger boy who was at risk of care or custody because of the number of his offences of theft. By the age of 14 he had built up a substantial record. His parents, his school, the community home he had lived in, social services, child guidance and the schools' psychological service, had all endorsed the programme offered. His parents were separated and he was torn between supporting his father who would otherwise live alone, and being with his mother and part of the family life which she could provide. Meanwhile he was a persistent truant from school and everyone said that his delinquent behaviour was 'an escape route'.

His programme is interesting for several reasons. First of all it is based on Jason being received into care voluntarily, under Section 2 of the Child Care Act 1980, in order to give time to sort out the complicated family situation. Everyone was agreed on this course, which required no action or sanction from the Court, but it was important that the magistrates knew about its importance as part of the plan for Jason.

Next, the Centre was able to prescribe for Jason a dose of community service as 'a substantial element of punishment'. Such arrangements for 14 year-olds are difficult to make. Not all 16 year-olds, let alone 14 year-olds, are mature enough to undertake the commitment of community service. They need more than the limited supervision available for those on many statutory schemes. That is one reason why 16 is the minimum age for the making of a Community Service Order as a disposal of the Court. Another is that most younger offenders have few skills that are useful to the community. Even clearing or tidying wasteland sites, weeding gardens for old people or basic home decorating, require a modicum of organizing ability and experience. Community service was feasible as part of the plan for Jason in Surrey through the siting of the official community service for 16 year-olds at the Centre. There was a pool of suitable jobs available through this and supervision suitable for younger boys. All the Centre's young people, whether on a Community Service Order, a supervised activities scheme or an intensive community programme, are constantly supervised with no more than three to a group.

Finally, the Centre took on the role of co-ordinating the work of the many agencies involved in Jason's life, including the task of finding appropriate education for him. 'It is about time', the Centre's report says, 'that the stated object of many previous Reviews since Jason has been known to Social Services of finding appropriate education is dealt with. . . . At the age of 14, he is still young enough to benefit from appropriate educational provision provided it can be sorted out now.' In addition, the Centre is able to offer art therapy: 'The purpose of this is to build upon the one area which Jason feels he is good at in school, at the same time addressing his deep-rooted anxieties and frustrations'. The programme thus demonstrates the breadth and flexibility of the Centre's work through its partnership with other agencies as well as its own resources.

In projecting these programmes and convincing courts of the validity of its approach, the Centre clearly has to make sure that the courts understand what takes place in the various sessions which are named. In addition, it is crucial to explain what will happen if such a detailed schedule as Jim's is breached. What if Jim does not turn up once, or twice? What if he is rude to his supervisor on placement or leaves an untidy mess behind him in the garden of the old person whom he is supposed to be helping? Not surprisingly with these young people there are a number of breaches, about 30 per cent of community service orders and 10 per cent of other requirements. The Centre is swift and tough in its reaction, bringing the young person back to court. What at first blush is surprising, is that by bringing the breaches back to court the Centre is sure it strengthens the confidence of the magistrates in its work. Instead of reacting by saying 'you've flagrantly disobeyed the court order. Therefore we must teach you a lesson by giving you another punishment', the Court sends them back to complete the Order, repeatedly if necessary. Sometimes straight admonishments will be effective. Sometimes a variation of extra days is made, or a small fine is imposed but the underlying assumption of all concerned is that part of the treatment – and punishment – is completing the course. It is the same philosophy that argues for repeating alternatives to custody rather than continuing up a tariff. The Centre also says that if the breach is brought to court early enough, the plan will not have yet broken down.

Liaison and expectations

One of the characteristics of the JORC is its full and clear documentation of all its processes. It aims to communicate well with everyone concerned. We have seen one aspect of its approach in the detailed assessment reports and suggestions for orders with which it presents courts. The same method of spelling out exactly what will happen, why, and when, is used for all the other parties involved, from the young person to the parents, the social workers, schools, landladies, and programme workers.

To start at the beginning of the Centre's involvement in a case, here is a typical letter sent to parents inviting them to take part in family therapy sessions.

Dear Mr and Mrs . . .
I am writing to you at the request of . . .'s Probation Officer, . . .
We had a meeting last week to see what method of work we could offer which would be likely to be of most help in . . . 's case. We finally decided that the best thing to do would be to meet with *all* of you as a family and talk things over.

We would like to ask you, as individuals and as a family, what the difficulties are that you face; how you have tried so far to tackle them; and to make a start on sorting out some solutions. To make a proper start on this it is very important that all of you should be present.

Could I suggest a time? Would . . . on . . . day, ..., be convenient? It helps if we can start and finish promptly; I would suggest that the meeting last for just one hour. Could we meet at your house?

It was originally suggested that I bring along with me a colleague from this Centre. However, as . . . . is . . . 's Probation Officer and will be continuing to work with him it seems to make much more sense if s/he stays involved as I am sure you will agree.

Would you please telephone . . . [the Probation Officer] or me to confirm whether the arrangements I have made in this letter are suitable for you all.

Yours sincerely

Meetings with families may only entail passing on information and making sure that all the family understand what the young person will be doing at or through the Centre and the reasons for the programme. More often than not, however, the opportunity is taken to explore with the family their relationship with the young person and to see how this can be improved. The Team Manager at the Centre from its beginning had an interest and some training in family therapy. If necessary, outside therapists are brought in to work with a family and it is always made clear that this work, in which the young person is involved, is part of the young person's programme. Participation following negotiation with the family is compulsory, and seen as improving his or her welfare.

The liaison with the young person's supervising officer is crucial to the success of a programme. First of all, it is the supervising officer who carries the statutory responsibility for the execution of an order under the Children and Young Persons Act 1969. The Centre is only the agent through which the officer acts. Just as important, the supervising officer in most cases has entered the life of the young person before the Centre became involved and unlike the Centre will continue 'to advise, help and be a friend' after completion of the days specified for work through the Centre. The JORC is willing to respond if necessary to those who have attended formerly, but it does not see itself as a continuing part of their lives, an ever-present place for old boys and girls to drop by. Its role is to ensure a smooth transition to the next stage at the completion of an order.

There are a number of stages in the partnership between the Centre and the supervising officer. The expectations at each are spelt out by the Centre. The principal document is as follows:

JUVENILE OFFENDER RESOURCE CENTRE: LIAISON WITH PROBATION OFFICERS AND SOCIAL WORKERS

A. Liaison Responsibilities of Juvenile Offender Resource Centre Officers

1 *Formal Reports to the Field Supervisor* The Juvenile Offender Resource Centre Officer will provide the field supervisor with the following reports:
   (a) An assessment report at the end of the induction period i.e. after 3 or 4 weeks.
   (b) A final report, showing progress, areas of work addressed, areas of work still outstanding, with any material which may assist the field supervisor during the balance of the Supervision Order.
   (c) A progress report will be provided every three months where there is a long-term requirement.

2 *Other contacts* In addition, contact will be made with the field supervisor in person, by telephone or letter, to agree a response on every significant development but not less frequently than once each month.

3 *Co-working* In selected cases – particularly those on the Intensive Community Programme – co-work may be negotiated either as a feature of the Court Order, or in good practice terms.

B. Juvenile Offender Resource Centre: Expectations of the Field Supervisor

Either prior to Court or during the immediate post Court assessment period negotiations should take place between the field supervisor and the Juvenile Offender Resource Centre officer to agree:

(a) The regularity with which the field supervisor will require the offender to report.

(b) The circumstances under which the field supervisor will contact the Juvenile Offender Resource Centre officer (e.g. failure to report, family crisis, truancy etc).

(c) Meeting between the field supervisor, the Juvenile Offender Resource Centre Officer and the offender:
    (i) Towards the end of the first month of the order.
    (ii) For handover session at the conclusion of the Requirement.

C. This Minimum Standard of Liaison Activity is Endorsed by the Senior Managers Meeting 30 July 1987

These documents are not referred to as contracts but in some ways that is what they are, with obligations and responsibilities spelt out for all parties. The document given to the Supervising Officer concerning the meeting towards the end of the first month of the order gives more details of what is expected. 'The purpose of this meeting', it says, 'is to discuss response to the Programme at the Juvenile Offender Resource Centre and the Supervision Order. At this meeting we will be providing a written report on progress, and would like to have your comments on response to your own supervision under the following headings.' The headings given are: Attendance/punctuality, Focus of supervision, Family, Peers, Social Activities, Income, Additional comments on home/accommodation/work/school/unemployment/Juvenile Offender Resource Centre programme, and Areas that could be considered within supervision.

The programmes

What actually happens to a young person on a programme scheduled by the Centre? What does he or she do in the group meetings, in family and in individual sessions? How are work and instruction arranged on the pre-employment package?

Most of the young people attend group sessions at the Centre on two evenings a week from 4.30 to 8.00 pm. Towards the end of their programmes, attendance is reduced to one evening a week to counteract any tendency to dependency on the Centre and prepare young people for when their order has finished. The sessions are in the evening to avoid undermining school attendance for those of school age, or work for those in employment or on training schemes. On any one evening there are on average eight young people at the Centre and the largest number to have attended on any one evening is 17.

A member of the Centre team, or one of the sessional workers the Centre employs for specific projects, picks up by car those who are due for the evening. The Centre is on the outskirts of Woking but the young people come from all over Surrey. Some form of transport is essential for them as the bus service linking the towns and villages is poor. In this prosperous area most people have cars and the local transport system has suffered through lack of demand. Those who need it are not good at putting forward their case vociferously. In fact the workers at the Centre find they learn a lot about their young people during car journeys and also have a captive audience.

Punctuality is rigorously enforced but each session begins gently with a cup of tea for all. This is followed by an hour of sport, normally basketball. The Centre is a former children's home, a mainly two-storey building with one long room big enough for groups and a few smaller offices for individual work. It is set in grounds adjoining playing fields, so there is a sense of space and the outdoors. Staff play the game with the young people and say that even those who hated sport at school come to enjoy it. The game is played hard. As well as using up teenage energy the staff say it has a function as a safe outlet for violence.

At 6.15 p.m., after a break of a quarter of an hour for orange juice, they divide into groups of two to four for what is termed 'the correctional curriculum'. This means examining their offending behaviour, whether by reconstructing their actual offence, why it happened and its consequences for everyone, or looking in general at the reasons for and results of offending. They use role play to enact situations, to show the pressure to offend from friends or from frustration, and to demonstrate the effects on victims and families, with everyone trying to imagine what it is like for the others and reacting spontaneously. They watch videos with scenarios for comment. They do paper and pencil exercises, quizzes and games, according to the abilities and needs of each group. The workers cull ideas from works like *Offending Behaviour, Skills and Stratagems for Going Straight* by James McGuire and Philip Priestley, (the book most often cited by the projects seen for this study), or invent new approaches. Sometimes an outsider, like a policeman or magistrate, comes to talk and be questioned about his or her job.

At 7.15 p.m. supper is served, prepared by a member of the group and a supervisor on a rota basis. Each group collects its meal, eats the meal in its own room and then takes back the plates for the duty cook to wash up. The group then completes its exercises and discusses the evening's work. Everyone leaves between 7.50 p.m. and 8.10 p.m. and is usually taken home as he or she came.

The additional, individual counselling sessions are at the heart of the programmes offered by the Centre. The Centre has a limited, clearly defined primary aim, to reduce the use of custody and care, but it also exists as an element in Surrey's strategy to reduce offending. Recurrent crime may be curbed by various means which reflect its various causes. Effective intervention to prevent crime may include providing jobs and accommodation as well as improving the skills and changing the attitude of the individual. Argument continues about which means are best or whether the simplest answer is not minimal intervention since most young people grow out of crime. Although the role of the Centre is to serve the courts by offering a punishment in place of custody, nevertheless it has a strong strand of welfare woven into its approach. Its intervention in the life of a young person may be brief but the workers at the Centre believe that in a few cases a brief intervention at the right time may be effective. Moreover, their methods are geared to act as a foundation for further work if it is necessary, by others or on occasion by themselves. They have successfully offered short programmes of 10, 15, 20 and 25 days to suit individual needs.

Each young person has a key worker who uses many of the same methods as with groups, to face the individual with the issue of offending. The difference from groupwork is that the starting point is the young person's particular case. Thus if drinking is a problem for a 16 year-old and most of his offending took place when he was intoxicated, his drinking can be a focus for his work. He may be asked to keep a drink diary from which he and his worker can construct graphs that can be coloured in that show the time spent drinking and what it costs. The main emphasis is on teaching social skills: how to say 'no' without losing face or giving offence, whether to friends, family or strangers.

The effectiveness of work like this is based on accurate assessment of the young person's current position, skills and aims in life. To find out what is needed the young person and the worker co-operate. The young person thus has a hand in shaping his or her own programme and in modifying it at every stage, whether it is progressing well and so may need accelerating or expanding, or whether it is not proving helpful and needs changing. If the worker has not the precise skills necessary to meet some aspect of the course devised, the Centre may employ a sessional worker who has the necessary experience. This method of working may sound cumbersome but it brings with it much more likelihood of acceptance and understanding by the young person. It also teaches young people useful skills of negotiation and the value of discussion and planning. Standardized tests of social adjustment are used and the results always shared with the young person. One schedule of questions found particularly useful is that devised by Dr Eugene Heimler in *Survival in Society* to measure how the respondent feels about himself, his life and other people. The answers form a base against which to chart progress over the months.

Here is a set of questions filled in by Gary, a 16 year-old who reoffended while on a 60-day intensive community programme at the Centre. As part of his individual programme he was learning skills to make him more assertive. Although he wanted to have a gregarious, macho image, he was in reality anxious and introverted. The programme would help him to identify his own strengths so that he would have less need to compensate in an anti-social way. The magistrates were given the piece of work reproduced below and his supervisor's report for the session when he reappeared in court, in order to show that some progress had been made with Gary and more was possible. The supervisor was also in court to answer any questions the magistrates wanted to ask.

The sheet is headed 'Transition Scrapbook'. Transition in this context refers to adolescence in general as a period of transition as well as specific transitions like those from school to work, and on leaving home. The exercises help to identify whether young people have the skills to handle the changes they will face and to show where they need help. The questions are on the left and Gary's answers on the right.

Previous transition	*Social work*
What do I remember?	*Sessions*
How was I different afterwards?	*Aware of dangers (consequences)*
Did it cause me any difficulty?	*No*

Did anything or anybody help?	*Staff*
If so – how?	*Made me aware*
Current transition	*Intensive community programme*
What am I moving from and to?	*Moving from nothing to further sessions*
How was I before?	*Free*
How am I becoming different?	*Clearer in my mind*
What is difficult about the stage I am at?	*Nothing*
What could I do that would help?	*Don't know*
What advantages will there be for me in what is ahead?	*No trouble further or extra*
Future transition	*Court*
What will I move from?	*Freedom*
What will I move to?	*Possible DC [Detention Centre]*
How will I behave differently?	*Depressed, anger*
What difficulties may there be?	*Obeying authority*
How can I help myself or get help?	*Don't know*
What will I miss or lose?	*Family, friends, job, freedom*
What will I gain?	*Don't know*
Is this transition something I want to happen?	*No*
Am I somebody who 'makes things happen' rather than sits back and lets things happen (i.e. do I know what I want and make efforts to achieve it?)	*No (easily led)*
Do I know what I would like to get out of this new situation?	*Another chance to prove myself*
Do I know what I do not want from this new situation?	*DC*
If I feel under stress do I know what I can do to help myself?	*No (revolt?)*
Do I know how I will be expected to behave in a new situation?	*Yes*
Is there any way I can 'try out' the new situation?	*Yes, prepare myself (rehearse evidence)*
Do I know other people on whom I can depend in a crisis?	*Parents*
with whom I can discuss concerns?	*Family*
to whom I feel close (a friend)?	*Cousin*
who can recognize my strengths and make me feel values?	*No (rejection)*

who can give me the information I need?	*Probation worker, social worker*
who will challenge me and make me face things I need to face?	*Don't know*
with whom I can share good times and experiences?	*Cousin*
Do I get regular exercise or have a keep-fit programme?	*No*
Do I eat regularly and sensibly?	*Yes*
Do I know when and how to relax?	*Yes*
Do I follow a regular routine?	*Partly (work only)*
Do I have places, people or situations which give me a 'secure base'?	*Home, relatives*
Do I give myself a treat if I am going through a bad patch?	*Yes*
Do I have people who will 'take care' of me at times when I need them?	*Parents*
Am I able to 'survive' (i.e. keep myself going during times that are hard until the better times come?	*Didn't but will (determination)*
Do I know the times and situations when I am likely to be at my lowest?	*Yes*
Do I 'hang on' to what is past or easily leave one situation and move to another?	*Both – dependent on degree*
Do I often think 'it's not fair, this should not happen to me'?	*Yes*
Do I want to 'get through' the bad patches, leave the past behind and carry on with what lies ahead?	*Yes*
Am I able to find opportunities to express anger or other strong feelings in ways that help?	*Yes*
Am I able to find at least one thing that I have gained by moving in to my new situation?	*Awareness of consequences*
Am I able to list various opportunities I now have which I didn't have or hadn't thought of before?	*No*
Have I learned something new about myself? If so, what?	*No*

Am I able to describe the ways in
which I am different from how I
was before?   *More aware (of consequences)*

What have I learned that will be
useful in future?   *Crime doesn't pay*

In describing a lifeskills session, which lasted an hour and a half, Gary's supervisor wrote that the purpose of the session was 'to explore further positiveness and assertiveness'. He described Gary's mood as 'happy', one of 12 adjectives offered for selection, including sullen, troubled, irritable and neutral. His behaviour, level of interest, response, attention, participation in discussion and the quality of his work are rated in the middle of a scale of five, with the relevance of the material to the individual rated slightly higher. The supervisor makes as his 'key statement': 'Gary was fully co-operative, attentive and appeared interested. He took part in discussion without prompting and was more forthcoming than before.' He comments further that assertive and non-assertive behaviour was fully discussed, as were the resulting consequences. 'Freedom of choice of action was discussed and the theory that any action is valid and acceptable, as long as it does not interfere with or distress others, was analysed.'

The concluding paragraph may have been instrumental in influencing the magistrates and persuading them to give Gary another chance but it was not written with the knowledge that they would see it. It read:

> During this session Gary was much more relaxed than before. He seemed eager to start work. At no time did he hedge. He faced everything squarely and, as far as I can tell, honestly. He was voluble and spoke freely, offering his own views in discussion. All in all, the change in Gary over these few sessions is quite dramatic. Should further sessions be made possible, and change and improvement continue in the same pattern, the hope of recovery and stabilization must be high. Of course, guarantees are impossible, but Gary is giving off signals of readiness for change and this is encouraging. To what extent this results from the immediate crisis of his court appearance it is difficult to assess but there are signs, deep under the surface, that Gary is beginning to think for himself, and this must be a first step towards change.

The report on his community service placement, doing removals, was also favourable and Gary was given his chance of a further intensive community programme for 60 days, to include a programme of social lifeskills related to offending. He was also to participate in family meetings and to undertake individual work as directed by his officer. These activities would take 25 days, community service 16 days, and a community placement 19 days. The sessional worker who was trained in using the transitions exercise was to carry out the lifeskills work with Gary.

The skills taught on the pre-employment scheme include market gardening (producing plants), general building work, carpentry, electrics, labouring, motor and cycle repairs. Priority for places is given to the most serious offenders and those for whom it is part of their specified programmes as an alternative to custody or care. The young people must either be over 16 and unemployed or in the last two terms of school age. Those in their last two terms of school will often have no prospect of being accepted again in a regular school and so the scheme cannot be said to take young people who have a viable chance of returning to mainstream education. As in all the work the Centre undertakes, the objectives are agreed with everyone concerned, with the head teacher for those of school age, as well as with the young person, parents and social worker. All parties, and the Education Department when appropriate, are informed in writing at the acceptance stage of the young person's attendance on the programme, and the proposed or negotiated arrangements for future placement on leaving the programme. Although it is emphasized that the pre-employment group is for a limited time period, extended only in exceptional circumstances, provision for the future is built into the project. The document describing the scheme continues as follows:

> At the commencement of the programme an assessment takes place with the youngster to negotiate a curriculum for a six week period before reassessment.
>
> At this stage the Home Tutor will be involved to assess the educational aspects. It is expected that the Educational Department would meet their obligations under the 1944 and 1982 Acts in the educational support necessary. This educational support, if appropriate, should be provided through the Home Tutor Service rather than by an employee of the Social Services Department or a permanently seconded teacher. The reason for the use of the Home Tutor Service is that in all cases where the programme provides a holding operation, the youngster's return to mainstream education should constitute the future negotiated placement. Any additional service provided by the Education Department should be directed towards this end.
>
> **Duration of Programme**
> (i)   The programme operates in six-week blocks with a review period at the end of six weeks.
> (ii)   A close down for one week at the end of each six-week block will be for the purpose of assessing priorities, needs and developments for each youngster in line with policy and practice. This will include review of the plans for further placement of the youngster at the conclusion of the placement.

Content of Programmes
(i)   Following the initial referral and gatekeeping process, the Scheme commences with an induction comprising assessment leading to a negotiated programme.
(ii) The content of the programme is intended to meet educational, social skills, and work training needs identified at the assessment stage. It is also designed to prepare the youngster for a future placement identified at the beginning of the programme.

Monitoring, Evaluation and Assessment
(i)   A report is written on each client at the end of each week. This is sent to
(a)   Juvenile Offender Resource Centre officer if appropriate and/or
(b)   Supervising Officer.
One copy remains on file.
(ii) It is also hoped that Personal Records of Achievement can be adopted in future either in addition to or instead of (i) above. This would be of four-fold benefit:
(a)   For a youngster whose chief aim is to return to school, a Personal Record of Achievement completed during his absence from mainstream education will enable him to leave school with a complete and full record since it can be incorporated into the overall profile.
(b)   For a youngster for whom a return to mainstream education is not possible, a Personal Record of Achievement can be completed. He/she will, therefore, not be denied the opportunity of this new development in education.
(c)   The benefits of the Personal Record of Achievement for all clients of school age must be of similar importance to unemployed juveniles attending the Scheme. There seems to be no reason why unemployed clients should not also complete Records of Achievement.
(d)   Records of Personal Achievement can, therefore, form the basis of monitoring and evaluating youngsters' achievements in accordance with national criteria.

Management Structure and Supervision
(i)   The Pre-Employment group as a constituent scheme of the Juvenile Offender Resource Centre is managed by the Team Manager who is accountable to the Inter-agency Officers' Steering Group and the joint member level committee which includes both chief officer and member representation from the Education Department.
(ii) Within the Juvenile Offender Resource Centre the structure is as follows:
(a)   One officer of the Centre is responsible for the day-to-day management of the scheme including supervision of three sessional workers and a volunteer.

(b) One officer of the Centre (a former teacher) is responsible for the development of provision including liaison with the Education Department. As this officer is female she is responsible for any necessary counselling sessions with girls referred to the scheme. Formal supervision sessions with the sessional workers take place twice a week; developmental meetings attended by all workers and the Team Manager take place on a monthly basis.

The residential element

Many of the programmes put forward by the Juvenile Offender Resource Centre contain a residential element. Young people may be sent for a week to an outward bound type of course, for example at one of the centres specializing in such courses in Wales. For Jim, a spell away from his locality was thought appropriate at the beginning of his sentence, to give him and everyone else a short break which marked a change in his circumstances. However, the period spent away from home, perhaps walking on the fells in the Lake District, working on a National Trust or other conservation scheme, joining a tall ships sailing course, going to an army cadet corps camp or helping at a holiday camp run by PHAB (the Physically Handicapped/Able Bodied organization), may come at any appropriate stage. Sometimes the young people are sent to join a specific course on their own but the staff at the Centre take the most difficult young people themselves. It is important to ensure that the experience is a good one for the young person, testing him or her in new surroundings and opening up new possibilities.

Residential trips for young offenders have often been criticized in the press as 'jaunts' on the rates, or holidays for the undeserving. Why should a boy who has seriously wounded a policeman go mountain-climbing in Wales when his law-abiding neighbour has never travelled beyond Guildford? Professional workers in child care have also grown sceptical in recent years about the value of taking young people for a short period out of their usual environment. How can experiences in a totally different context be applied at home? If a major argument against custody is that it does not help the young to face choices and to change their life-style at home, could not the same be said of climbing hills?

The workers at the Juvenile Offender Resource Centre take a similar view to many of the early proponents of Intermediate Treatment. The authors of the report *A Future for Intermediate Treatment*, published by the Personal Social Services Council in 1977, considered a residential element an important first stage in any scheme. At the Centre, they think it helpful for young people to taste alternatives and emphasize that exposure to new experiences can be extremely taxing. The kind of course which middle class people might consider a holiday is often terrifying for a boy or girl who has never been away from his or her own locality, perhaps even from home. It is easy to forget that holidays are beyond the budgets of many of their families. In addition, on these excursions they learn a little about community living, the need to co-operate and to share. It also creates opportunities for adults and young people to learn more about each other and to achieve objectives together.

Management and costs

The management structure of the Juvenile Offender Resource Centre was crucial to its development and is crucial to its success. The Centre has its roots in collaboration between the probation and social services. To these agencies was added representation from the youth services, the magistracy, the justices' clerks and the police. The range of participation is reflected in the professional backgrounds of the workers at the Centre where the Team Manager is a former probation officer and the staff include former teachers, residential care workers and people with youth and community as well as social work qualifications and degrees. The full degree of collaboration rather than mere liaison is ensured by the membership of the Surrey Care Trust Board of chief officers, including the Director of Social Services, the Chief Constable, the Chief Probation Officer and, perhaps a key figure, the County Treasurer. The line of management runs from the Board of Management, to the Management Committee, to the Officers' Steering Group, to the team at the Centre. Membership in 1988 was as follows:

Board of Management
7 Members appointed by the Probation Committee
1 Member appointed by Surrey County Council
2 Members appointed by the Chief Probation Officer
2 Members appointed by the Director of Social Services
1 Member appointed by the Chief Constable
The Chief Probation Officer
The Chief Constable

The Director of Social Services
The Secretary of the Trust = Chief Executive
The Treasurer of the Trust = County Treasurer
Between one and three members appointed by the Trust

Management Committee
Two JPs
Chairmen, Social Services and Probation Committees
Assistant Chief Probation Officer
Assistant Director and an Area Director, Social Services
A Chief Superintendent, Surrey Constabulary
Deputy County Youth Adviser
Chairman, Justices' Clerks Society
Team Manager attends, as do clerks' and Treasurer's representatives

Officers' Steering Group
Assistant Chief Probation Officer
Assistant Area Director and Development Officer, Social Services
Youth and Community Services Officer
Team Manager attends

The commitment of the principal agencies is ensured by the fact that they contribute resources. Originally the Probation Service gave £49,000 per annum to include the funding of two professional staff posts and administrative support. Social services gave £89,600 per annum for three professional staff posts and administrative support. The money received through the Surrey Care Trust from the DHSS 1983 funding initiative, was £90,000 for four professional posts and administrative support. After a six months' extension of the DHSS funding, the continuation of the Juvenile Offender Resource Centre after August 1987 was agreed by probation continuing its former level of funding and social services contributing the residue.

Balance sheets of putative expenditure and savings are crude measures of all that is involved but there are obvious savings to both central and local government through the numbers of young people the Centre has been able to divert from custody or care. The figures produced by the Centre (Table 1) show that central government benefits from the reduction in the number of young people sent to detention centres or custody, from 63 in 1982 to 10 in 1987. The weekly cost of a place in open

COUNTY OF SURREY 1982–7: PROJECTIONS

Using 1982 figures as a base, a projection of the numbers who would have received custody or care (7/7) disposals in subsequent years had alternatives not been available; with estimated savings.

	Would have received custody	Actual custody	Would have received care (7/7)	Actual Care numbers (7/7)	Cost per head per week: custody (open)	Cost per head per week: Care – The Oaks excluding capital costs	Custody savings per week	Care savings per week	JORC weekly total costs
1982	63	63	31	31	231	387	–	–	–
1983	55	53	27	20	262	407	524	2,849	
1984	57	36	28	18	294	428	6,174	4,280	
1985	53	19	26	5	320	450	10,880	9,480	
1986	54	18	26	6	345	475	12,420	9,500	
1987	50	10	24	4	363	500	14,520	10,300	5,192

NOTES: 1. The 1987 figures show that the net weekly savings for the County, after allowances for the cost of JORC, are £5,108. Additional weekly savings of £14,520 accrue to the Home Office, making a total weekly saving of £19,628.

2. Average 1987–8 cost of a place at The Oaks Community Home is £40,967, (Chart. Inst. Public Finance and Accountancy figures: total cost divided by average occupancy) and of JORC is £6,900. On this basis, each diversion from Care (7/7) saves the County £34,067.

3. These figures do not show the substantial additional savings effected by diversion from Care of non-offenders by JORC (e.g. in Educational Care Proceedings).

4. Not shown here of course are the non-financial benefits accruing to young people, their families, and their local communities by the provision of alternatives to care and custody.

TABLE 1 *Estimated savings from alternatives to custody and care*

custody is calculated at £363 for 1987. Local authorities bear the costs of children and young people in their care so they benefit directly if offenders are given Supervision Orders with requirements for specified activities in the community rather than Care Orders. The weekly cost of a place in the local community home was £500 in 1987. More offenders are ordered into custody rather than care and it is a continuing, justifiable complaint of local authorities that this division of responsibility is arbitrary and unfair. In financial terms, central government benefits more than local authorities from alternatives in the community for offenders but the Centre calculates that in 1987 it saved a total of £24,820. If 50 young people had been sent into custody that would have cost central government £14,520 more, and if 24 had been sent into care that would have cost the local authority £10,300. The weekly running costs of the Centre are £5,192 so the net savings for the County are £5,108.

The same tight rein on setting and meeting goals governs the work of the team at the Centre, as applies to the young people, their families and their colleagues in other agencies. The 13 professional staff (including the four members of the Accommodation Scheme) and the administrative staff meet for two hours each week. In addition, every six weeks the Centre is closed, except for attendance at court and intensive community programmes which cannot be interrupted, while staff training and self-assessment takes place, of sessional workers as well as the permanent staff.

One week they might examine together their work on court reports. Were their own reports satisfactory to the court? Were their recommendations well argued and did they usually convince the magistrates or the judges at the Crown Court? The Crown Court deal with the most serious cases but the judges may be less familiar than magistrates with alternatives to custody in Surrey. Were local social workers availing themselves of the expertise at the Centre to help them write cogent reports?

Another week they might examine the role of the new Crown Prosecution Service and ensure that its officers knew about the functions of the Centre. Family therapy might be the focus on another occasion. Although a second member of staff always acts as a consultant when formal family therapy begins, in order to help the worker avoid being sucked into the family's web of concerns, outside experts are not often used. The Centre staff have found that this is a method of working they can practise if they add some specific training in it to their social work skills. Staff also attend external courses on various aspects of their work.

Every six months the team meets a facilitator to discuss major professional issues like re-organization in response to changing demand. The Team Manager sees all staff individually once every three weeks and each month attends a meeting of the various small teams into which the staff are divided to cover different aspects of the work. One such team carries the day-to-day management of the Surrey Accommodation Scheme. Even though this is a resource for the whole county for probation and social services clients between the ages of 16 and 19, two officers from the Centre supervise the two probation accommodation officers and the two social services officers who run it. They in turn are accountable through the JORC Team Manager to the Officers' Steering Group.

In 1987 the Centre established a Crime Prevention Team of two officers, to run community-based projects co-operatively with social workers, probation officers, youth workers, the police and others, in order to provide leisure, work experience and work for young people who had been before the courts. Their role included responsibility for the Pre-Employment Group. They had a clear focus, distinct from that of those offering the alternatives to custody and care. The Centre was thus able to become more involved in community work. An interesting aspect of this development was that it attracted charitable funding so that the money the Centre invested was increased by others.

Monitoring

The Juvenile Offender Resource Centre is essentially part of the wider provision in Surrey for juveniles and offenders. It was seen from the outset that its effectiveness could only be judged in relation to the system as a whole. Information was needed not only on the young people who attended the Centre but also on those who did not. It was decided to monitor continuously all disposals in Surrey courts and to employ the specialist consultancy service Social Information Systems, initially on a two-year contract, to analyse the data and to make recommendations arising from it. They were paid £9,450 + VAT a year, to cover the initial setting-up costs, including the provision of a computer and software, analysis of results and the production of two reports a year, and eight consultancy visits a year and other consultancy discussions.

The advantages of using this specialist expertise were several. First, facts about referrals and outcome were essential, both for their own planning and for public relations. Second, experienced consultants knew the right questions to ask, facts to collect and links to look for. Third, they would be able to set the Surrey experience in a national context. Social Information Systems have pioneered the idea of looking at the inter-action between different elements in the juvenile justice system. The service was set up by Professor Norman Tutt of the University of Lancaster, Dr D. H. Thorpe, M. D. Milan and Dr Henri Giller, who is its Director. All are well known for their contributions to criminology and their interest in juvenile offending. In the document they offer social services departments as their proposal to monitor and evaluate a juvenile justice system, they explain that many of the programmes aiming to develop alternatives to custody and care have tended to increase the numbers of young people in the system by offering specialist services inappropriately. This process is often called net-widening.

An effective information system can collect all the variable elements, from the ages and offences of the juveniles, to the recommendations in the reports by the social workers, to the disposals given by the courts. It can then analyse the material and pick out any connections, chart changes in the delinquent population and in the services provided, and recommend action to fulfil the aim of keeping young offenders in the community while avoiding net-widening.

The Surrey computer on which the information is filed is housed at the Centre and the Centre's staff key in the data using a software package supplied by the consultants. The eight variables collected on the characteristics of offenders are: the social services area where the young person lives, age at prosecution, sex, most serious offence under consideration by the court, number of previous police cautions, number of previous court sentences, most severe previous sentence, and the juvenile court passing the sentence. On types of official response there are three variables: the authorship of the social inquiry report, the recommendation of the social inquiry report and the juvenile court sentence. The data are analysed and presented in relation to each social services area office to take account of local variations. Social Information Systems present a report every six months and discuss their recommendations for policy and operational changes in the light of this report. They will also, by mutual agreement, offer training to assist development where necessary.

The SIS report on changes in the Surrey juvenile justice system between 1985 and 1987 thus covers Surrey's cautioning procedures, as well as the numbers and characteristics of young people attending the

Juvenile Offender Resource Centre, and those given other disposals. It is immediately obvious that not all the variables in young people's backgrounds are covered. Information is not sought about their personal or family characteristics. The information is limited to what is required to monitor the juvenile justice system. There is no attempt to enter sociological territory or ask questions about factors which may or may not predispose to delinquency. We cannot find out, for example, if young people from single parent families were more or less likely to be thought amenable to supervision in social workers' reports, or even how many black children appeared before the courts. (The Centre keeps no separate statistics about racial or ethnic origin, although three Asian young people – Woking has had an Asian community for many years – one Afro-Caribbean boy and one Chinese boy had attended by mid-1987.)

The report makes it clear that the Juvenile Offender Resource Centre did, in its first two years, achieve its main aim of reducing the number of young people sent into custody or care in Surrey, and it did so without increasing the total number of young people in the system. The use of care and custody dropped to 4.5 per cent in the first year and to 3.3 per cent in the second, comprising only five Care Orders, one Charge and Control Order, 13 Detention Centre and one Youth Custody Order for the whole of Surrey. The report points out that the overall court population dropped significantly, from 768 cases in the first year to 610 in the second and that there was a sharp decline in offences of burglary, for reasons that needed further exploration. The proportion of boys of all ages dropped during the period, but the proportion of girls, especially older girls, increased. These are national trends, caused by many factors which should be more closely analysed. The total number of girls in court from 1 August 1986 to 31 January 1987 was 85, 9.6 per cent of all defendants.

Information about cautioning was not accurate enough but the proportion of persistent offenders with three or more previous convictions remained constant at about 10 per cent of the total. Although there had been an increase in the use of the fine as a disposal, magistrates in Surrey gave conditional discharges less often than the national average. The report recommends close examination of those cases in which custody was the disposal, and examination of reports with unclear recommendations or recommendations for custody.

A total of 277 young people received court disposals from August 1986 to January 1987 of whom 21 boys (three aged 14, seven aged 15, ten aged 16 and one 17 year-old) were directed to the Centre through Supervision

Orders with requirements for Intermediate Treatment, supervised activities, the intensive community programme or through Community Service Orders. Six had committed assaults for their last offence, six burglaries, three theft, six stealing and driving away cars together with other offences. When all the recommendations in social inquiry reports were collated, it was found that 75.8 per cent of recommendations in reports by social workers were adopted and 66.7 per cent of those in probation reports. However, of the ten recommendations for alternatives to custody in reports by social workers, nine were adopted, and of the 13 by probation, nine (69 per cent). Probation officers write reports on the older age-group and are therefore more likely to be dealing with more serious and persistent offenders who are more at risk of custody.

An additional study of the effectiveness of the Centre has shown that between 40 and 50 per cent of those who attended the Centre re-offended within two years. This figure compares well with the rate of over 80 per cent re-offending after custody, but it also demonstrates that reformation does not come overnight or even after a 90-day Specified Activities Order. Unfortunately, there are nationally no statistics which trace what happens to young offenders in the long term.

The police keep the records for offenders over the age of 17 and until recently there had been no attempt to collate records. In 1987 the Centre began a project with Surrey police to monitor statistics after the usual two-year period. The initial findings raise the re-offending rate to around 60–65 per cent but do not show the seriousness or frequency of the re-offending, factors which should be taken into consideration. Further findings of this project should be interesting.

Public relations

Good publicity has been crucial to the success of the Juvenile Offender Resource Centre. Alternatives to custody and care will be used only if they are understood. The people who must know in detail what they offer are not only the magistrates making disposals in the juvenile court and the judges who have been given jurisdiction over the most serious cases in the Crown Court. Almost the most important group are the social workers and probation officers who write reports to the court and must be conversant with all the facilities available in their area. Their duties do not end with a court appearance, as they will continue any supervision during and after the time-limited period spent as an alternative to custody. The public should also be well-informed about the purpose of projects like the Centre. After all, the young people are their sons and daughters, nieces and nephews, grandchildren, and neighbours. They may themselves be the victims of thefts, burglaries, vandalism and occasionally violence. In addition they may be able to offer reparative work or put a spare room to use through the Accommodation Scheme.

The Centre tackles the considerable task of informing these different groups vigorously and in a number of ways. The close liaison and detailed documentation with all parties concerning individual cases have been explained. The initial problem, however, is ensuring that new entrants to the various groups are briefed. To this end an open day is held at the Centre every month, mainly for social workers and probation officers but sometimes attended by magistrates. The Team Manager visits each of the juvenile benches every year, at one of their regular training meetings, and discussion meetings with magistrates are held at the Centre. All interested parties are sent the results of monitoring and evaluation. One of the main functions of the tiers of management is to ensure the circulation of up-to-date information.

As well as such general information, the courts are sent the final report on a young person at the end of the order. This is probably the most effective and honest way that the Centre can show what it does, its strengths and limitations. Here is the final report on a 16 year-old who had been on an intensive community programme for 70 days after over 100 offences of burglary and stealing. He also had to pay over £300 in compensation at £30 a month once he had left school. It was his third intensive community programme, the first two having been for 30 days each.

A. Summary of Progress in Groupwork Sessions

1 *Behaviour and participation in groups* Reserved, not prepared to give very much, Keith is very defensive of own position and able to hold it. He uses confrontation avoidance whenever possible, the main tactic being the adoption of the near-perfect and hence irreproachable response.

2 *Areas of work covered and response* Six sessions completed, the remainder transferred to inividual sessions for the reasons stated above. Keith finds it very difficult to talk about feelings and emotions – he will change the subject if possible. Keith wants to give the impression of being able to cope with social skills situations which, in fact, he finds extremely difficult.

3 *Response to staff/peers* Polite, chatty, liked by staff but owing to

points made above, groupwork staff felt unable to progress further within group situations on the necessary social skills and self-awareness needed.

B. Summary of Progress on Community Placements

1 *Type of work undertaken and response*
(a) Tuesday evenings: Physically Handicapped and Able Bodied Club.
(b) The Friends Anonymous Society, Hackney. This church-run charity for the elderly and homeless was affected by Keith's stealing money from one of its sponsor churches.

2 *Response to staff/peers*
– To 'give' something to those less fortunate than himself i.e. indirect reparation. Good response.
– To meet some victims of offending – direct reparation impractical in Hackney. Response – denied. Keith was unable to see how this particular piece of offending affected individuals living in East London.

C. Summary of Progress on Individual Sessions

1 *Areas of work covered and response*
(a) Heimler Scales of Social Functioning.
(b) Counselling and problem-solving with emphasis on self-awareness.

2 *Response to staff*
Very co-operative providing he was not threatened, when his politeness becomes a defence mechanism. The outcomes of these sessions stress the need for contact, containment, attention, and credibility (status). Money is associated with excitement and credibility.

3 *Additional comments*
Keith began to open up during the latter stages of the programme. Final evaluations using Heimler Scales and Lifeskills Transitions indicate that while life at present is better than it has been, is more in balance and more in control, there are long-term problems still to be addressed (see conclusion).

Keith has been able to initiate and maintain permanent positive changes himself; for example, getting a part-time job took over a year but now he is taking on other jobs in order to complete payment of fines by the target set.

The confidence gained by these opportunities in part contributed to the success of a job application in a tax office in the City and to a choice of career in the navy.

Keith is an achiever but targets set often very high and difficult to attain, i.e. still tendency to leave things to chance rather than effort. Support is still needed in encouraging realistic targets, i.e. self-understanding and maintaining motivations. At present, he is concerned about the long term and the worthwhile – good. A career in the navy is realistic in terms of his needs and what he is able to offer but the competition for officers' training is considerable.

D. Family Meetings

Informal but regular meetings with Supervising Officer, Keith, Mother, Sister and JORC. The family needs to be encouraged to let Keith take responsibility for himself. His sister is good at this, Mum isn't. Keith is beginning to understand what family has got to offer him other than material/basic needs. He is not sure whether his family has prepared him for adult life or what he is able to offer the family. (All areas for future work.)

E. Summary of Progress on Community Service

1 *Placement attended*

Saturdays Old people's home. Good reports but objections were raised by neighbours about Keith doing voluntary work there. This forced the owners to end the placement although they were reluctant to do so.

Weekends/holidays Gardening for the elderly and disabled. Residential project for disadvantaged in Surrey. Maintenance of graveyard at church from which he stole.

Sundays As above. National Trust and English Heritage renovation project.

2 *Purpose of placement and response*

Popular with staff. Able to work with the minimum of supervision. Found work tiring especially since the time he began working fulltime and on Saturdays. Some direct reparation was completed for the church; indirect reparation for the elderly from whom he also stole.

F. Summary of Progress on Residential

Keith's residential days were cancelled for the following reasons: Enforcement of a residential towards the end of this programme would have broken into patterns of work being established and cut across Keith taking on responsibility for the payment of fines and compensation. The purpose of a residential placement for Keith as an away from home challenging experience was seen as less likely to address social development than the new work situations Keith was adapting to and the encouragement that could be given to Keith in organizing his own visit to relatives in France.

Eight residential days were converted to:

(a) Weekend Community Service at the church and National Trust (6 days)

(b) Two individual sessions

[The wording of Keith's order had allowed residential days to be used for other purposes at the discretion of the supervising officer, so it had not been necessary to return to court to ask permission for the changes.]

Overall Summary and Additional Comments

Keith has not offended since an incident with a shopping trolley a year ago. Whether he re-offends or not in the future will probably be weighed against how much he's got to lose. Particularly vulnerable times are likely to be the next three months. Keith feels he has passed the transition between boredom/offending and 'becoming adultish' and says he is looking towards a solid career and future since he has written 'I don't want to be a criminal all my life'.

Suggested Areas for Future Work

Work Navy, college, 6th form.

Leisure Friendships.

Conclusion We have known Keith for a year and eight months and since that time we have seen quite a considerable change take place. Keith himself says the programmes have given him time to sort things out and certainly he has gained more confidence and some understanding of himself and his relationships with others. He is now taking full responsibility for his past and present behaviour and completed the last 70 days in excellent style.

Key features

The personality and ability of the leader of any project are key factors in its success. Although the structure of the Juvenile Offender Resource Centre in Surrey is one of its most important features, it has undoubtedly been shaped from the beginning by John Dixon, the Team Manager. A former probation officer who trained at the London School of Economics in his mid-twenties, after reading classics at Cambridge, he has clearly stamped his clarity of purpose, enthusiasm and efficiency on the project. The staff, at first all male but by 1987 including three women, like most of those who work in Intermediate Treatment are impressive as individuals and as a group. The contribution of individuals will always vary but the other key features of the Juvenile Offender Resource Centre which have been described can be summarized:

• The project began with a clean slate since Intermediate Treatment facilities in Surrey had previously been rudimentary.

• There was nevertheless a tradition of co-operation between social services and probation and of interest from the magistracy.

• The inter-agency co-operation was integrated into the juvenile justice system by giving the Centre responsibility for reports, advice, community service, accommodation and other services for juveniles.

• The top managers in the agencies are involved in the project. This ensures that it is understood as part of the juvenile justice system and services for children and young people in Surrey.

• Although the scope of the project is wide, its aims are narrow and clear.

• The credibility of the project as an alternative to custody has been sustained by its ability to offer appropriate training in skills and reparative work in the community.

• The problem of alternative housing for young people unable or unwilling to live at home has been tackled in such a way as to avoid reception into care in some cases.

• There is constant communication between all the people involved, with clear definition of their roles, written agreements about the distribution of work and feed-back about results.

• The project is able to buy in expertise on a sessional basis.

• Time for training is set aside regularly.

• The system is professionally monitored so that both assessment of performance and planning for the future have a factual basis.

• Young people are told clearly why they are at the Centre. Its purpose and limitations are made plain to them. They are involved in shaping their own programmes and assessing their own progress.

3

Contracts and Race in the Inner City
The Junction Project, London Borough of Lambeth

It would be hard to find an area which contrasted more starkly with Surrey than the London Borough of Lambeth, where the Junction Project for intensive Intermediate Treatment opened its doors in 1981. According to the most recent overall documentation about Lambeth, *Lambeth Facts & Figures 1985*, about a quarter of households in Lambeth had gross incomes at the time of the 1981 census of less than £3,000 a year. Lambeth had the highest number of unemployed people of all London boroughs, with 22 per cent of the population aged over 16 claiming supplementary benefits in July 1984. As in most London boroughs, the population was declining in numbers and ageing but Lambeth had the second highest proportion of all London boroughs of people aged 16 to 24.

The other distinctive feature of Lambeth is its black population. In total about a quarter of residents are from ethnic minorities, and in Brixton, about 40 per cent. Just over 60 per cent of ethnic minority residents are of West Indian origin but 90 per cent of black children under 16 were born in the United Kingdom. In the 1981 census, which counted households where the head of the household was born in the New Commonwealth or Pakistan, Lambeth had the sixth highest proportion of black residents in the country. The age profile of the black population is much younger than that of the white population, with 45 per cent of the black population aged under 19, compared with 23 per cent of the white population. In 1985 nearly a third of school pupils in Lambeth were of West Indian origin.

Lambeth has been the subject of several studies in recent years, all of which, including the Scarman Inquiry into the Brixton Disorders (1981), have exposed the extent of poverty in the area. About a third of Lambeth families have only one parent, the highest proportion in the country according to the 1981 census, and one parent families are in every locality among the poorest groups. Only 26 per cent of West Indian and 14 per cent of Asian families are headed by lone parents but in general it is among the black population that deprivation is worst.

Ethnic differences are marked in the employment pattern with 62 per cent of people of West Indian origin doing manual work and only 2 per cent in managerial or professional posts, 20 per cent of Asian people doing manual work and 25 per cent in managerial or professional posts, and 40 per cent of white people doing manual work and 15 per cent in managerial or professional posts. Unemployment is highest among unskilled manual workers. In Brixton and Stockwell, where most people of West Indian origin live, one in three working men was looking for a job in 1986 and 10 per cent of Lambeth's unemployed were aged 18 and 19. There are no separate figures on the level of unemployment among black people in Lambeth but information at national level shows that unemployment rates are higher among black people, particularly those in the younger age groups.

Black households tend to occupy the borough's poorest quality housing and a higher proportion of black people live in overcrowded conditions. In 1985 they comprised almost a third of those on the waiting list for Council accommodation and 45 per cent of the homeless. Since 1979 targets have been set by the Council to ensure that black households receive a fair share of housing.

How does this level of deprivation affect young people? Lambeth is one of the London boroughs with the highest proportion of children in care, (18.58 per 1000 of the population under 18 on 31 March 1984), and nearly half of children in residential placements at that time were black, although efforts were being made to encourage formal fostering and adoption in the black community. As for crime, whatever is thought about the connection between deprivation and crime, the crime rate is likely to be high where the proportion of juveniles in the population is high, since most offences are committed by young people. In 1986 there were 1,119 completed juvenile court cases in Lambeth. The borough operated or sponsored 34 programmes for young people at risk in 11 establishments and had five specialist schemes, of which the Junction Project was the only facility specifically designed as an alternative to custody.

It is difficult to compare in a useful way the number of cases in different London boroughs. The volume of crime among juveniles has to be measured against their numbers in the population. The number of cases brought to court depends on variable factors like the cautioning rate in the area and whether there are multi-agency panels sifting cases. In Lambeth only a third of offenders were cautioned in 1986, compared with 39 per cent in neighbouring Southwark and 37 per cent in neighbouring Wandsworth. As there are no uniform criteria for cautioning we do not know how to account for these differences. Did fewer of those accused in Lambeth admit to the offences and therefore could not be cautioned? Or were their alleged offences too serious or their previous records too long to permit a caution?

The types of offences before the court can to some extent be compared. In Lambeth Juvenile Court during 1986, 18 per cent of cases were for assaults or robbery and 10 per cent for burglary. By contrast, Southwark had 13 per cent assault and robbery cases and 19 per cent burglary cases, and Wandsworth 12 per cent assault and robbery cases and 15 per cent burglary cases. The high proportion of serious cases containing an element of violence has obvious implications for the disposals made by courts. It is of prime importance in designing alternatives to custody. Yet even on these matters comparisons are difficult since the definition of what constitutes robbery rather than theft may vary from area to area.

The early years

The Junction Project opened in 1981 as a joint venture financed on a three-year agreement by the Department of Health and Social Security, (which contributed £60,000 a year), Lambeth Social Services (£20,000 a year) and Save the Children Fund (£20,000 a year). The Inner London Education Authority (ILEA) agreed to give Save the Children Fund grant-aid to employ two teachers. The Cicely Northcote Trust leased the project, at a concessionary rent, a building at the north-east end of the borough, close to St Thomas's Hospital and nearer Westminster than Brixton. Save the Children Fund managed the scheme.

This partnership between central government, the voluntary sector and a local authority was innovative and trend-setting. It was proposed after Julian Holder of Lambeth Social Services had read the report of the Personal Social Services Council, *A Future for Intermediate Treatment*, and asked the DHSS, where Norman Tutt, one of the contributors to the Report, was Principal Social Work Service Officer, if it would support in Lambeth an experimental intensive Intermediate Treatment project as advocated. This was the model adopted soon after in the 1983 DHSS

Intermediate Treatment initiative. The expectation for projects set up under the DHSS initiative was for them eventually to become the responsibility of the local area, a permanent part of its provision for young people, without central funding. In similar manner the Junction Project was handed over to Lambeth Social Services on 1 January 1985.

A detailed study of its first collaborative years, from October 1981 to December 1983, was published by the University of Surrey in November 1984, in *Intensive Intermediate Treatment for Persistent Young Offenders. A Study of the Junction Project.* Maureen Stone of the Department of Educational Studies at the University of Surrey conducted the research which was funded by the Cicely Northcote Trust. We thus have more information and evaluation than is usual about an Intermediate Treatment project, but the study described the Junction Project's first stages only. It is instructive to see how the Project has developed, what elements have remained the same and how it has been affected by changes of management.

From the outset the first Director of the Project, Martin Farrell, made a point of documenting and publicizing its work. Its first interim report, issued in November 1982 after the Project had been in operation for 18 months, has as its cover illustration a corner of a Monopoly game board in which the dreaded command 'GO TO JAIL' is changed to 'GO TO JUNCTION PROJECT'. The report explains:

> We will consider boys and girls who are resident in Lambeth, or for whom a Lambeth agency has responsibility, and who are over 12 years old but still under the jurisdiction of the juvenile court. We will only accept youngsters who have committed an offence which is likely to attract a custodial sentence or subsequent placement in residential care.
>
> We offer a 12 month programme for 48 youngsters in six groups of eight. Groups start every two months.
>
> During the first three months, youngsters attend the Project five days a week and on Saturday mornings. Following this, each youngster is expected to attend the Project one evening a week with other members of his/her group for a further period of three months. Thereafter there is a weekly 'drop-in' group which is open to all youngsters who have previously attended the Project.
>
> The first three months of the programme is clearly structured and [consists of] small group meetings, individual counselling sessions, community meetings, a midday meal prepared by the youngsters and daily discussion workshops covering areas such as law, education,

finding and keeping a job, health education and community service. The weekly evening groups run on similar lines and consist of group meetings and activities such as visits, use of video and group games. This long-term contact serves to follow youngsters' progress and to consolidate work already undertaken.

It is immediately clear that the Junction Project was from the beginning exclusively an alternative to custody or care, one of the first of its kind, determined not to widen its net and catch less serious offenders. At the outset it offered a set series of groups starting on predetermined dates to which individuals were allocated according to their dates of referral. Attendance was full-time for three months, even though some potential members were of school age and others had jobs. A formal follow-on was included and the whole process lasted a year. The main activities took place at the Project centre rather than in the locality.

The first interim report goes on to describe the referral procedure and the use of a contract between the four parties involved in a placement: the young person, the parent, the social worker who made the referral and the Project. From its early days the Project monitored the Lambeth court lists and offered to see, before their court appearance, any young people who might be at risk of being sent into custody because of the nature of their alleged offence or their previous record. The aim of such intervention was to give the young person and their family a clear idea of the purpose of the Project and what would be expected of them if the court permitted the young person to attend. Not all young people decided to proceed voluntarily at that stage nor could the Project monitor all Lambeth young people appearing in other London juvenile courts because they had committed offences in those areas. Although the usual practice in Inner London juvenile courts is to return young people to their home court for sentencing, on the grounds that the magistrates there will be more familiar with local provision, sometimes the court where the case has been resolved makes the disposal.

Copies of the contract, when agreed and signed by all parties, were presented to the court with a report from the Project giving details of what it could offer the individual. A member of the Project staff was normally in court to support the proposal despite the strain on staff resources of having to attend sometimes all three of Lambeth's court days each week, as well as other juvenile, adult and Crown Courts. The Project always made a recommendation about which disposal would allow them to proceed best. Before the advent of specified activities as a condition attached to a Supervision Order, it generally asked for sentence to be deferred for a period during which the young person might attend the Project. Thirty-one of the 50 young people attending the first seven groups run by the Project were on deferred sentences. Many of the young people were already the subject of Supervision Orders, sometimes with Intermediate Treatment requirements, or were already in Lambeth's care. It was thought that magistrates would be reluctant to repeat Supervision Orders or to make a Supervision Order if a Care Order was already in force.

The legal basis on which a court may defer a sentence is that there is a reasonably clear indication of change likely to occur in the offender's conduct or circumstances. The court therefore defers making its disposal to see the effect of any changes. The offender must agree to the deferment, which may be for a period of up to six months. The court gives its reasons for deferment and makes clear what it expects will happen during the period. The agreement is that if the offender does what is expected – it might be 'to keep out of trouble and to attend the Junction Project, bringing good reports back to court' – the disposal at the end of the period will not be severe. The magistrates making the deferment will not necessarily be (indeed in London are unlikely to be) the same as those who at the end of the period of deferment hear what has happened to the offender and make the final disposal. Although the first court cannot bind its successor about the ultimate disposal, suggestions like 'save up for a possible fine' indicate the kind of penalty to be expected if the offender toes the line. If young people re-offend during the period, they are brought back to court and punished immediately but they cannot be brought back for failing to fulfil expectations like attendance at the Project.

Now that specified activities can be ordered under a Supervision Order, with sanctions for breaking the conditions, the deferred sentence is a cumbersome means of trying to secure attendance at a project as an alternative to custody. However, before the option of specified activities was available, the deferred sentence could be an effective tool. It can also be argued that the offender under a deferred sentence is liable to several punishments, restrictions on his or her life-style in the period of deferment as well as a penalty at the end. Of the 26 young people on deferred sentences who completed the first seven groups run by the Project up to August 1982, eight were eventually conditionally discharged, six were fined, one was sent to an attendance centre, two were given Probation Orders, two Supervision Orders, two mixed disposals in the community and five, who had re-offended, were sent to detention centre or Borstal. Thus all those who kept out of trouble did escape custody.

Examples of the contracts first used were published in the interim Report. Although they were subsequently modified to reflect changes in the Project's programming, they were substantially the same in form in 1987. One semantic alteration in the young person's agreement was the change from 'I agree to try not to commit any further offences' initially, to 'I will not commit any more offences' by the end of 1984, to 'I agree not to commit any offences during my Intensive Supervision programme' in 1987.

Here are the four contracts used in 1987, before amendment for use under Supervision Orders with specified activities:

The Young Person

1 I want to take part in the Junction Project's Intensive Supervision programme.
2 I agree not to commit any offences during my Intensive Supervision programme.
3 I agree to take part in full in the programme that has been arranged with me (see attached details).
4 I agree to try to keep all appointments, to telephone the Junction Project if I am ill or unable to attend for any reason, or if I am going to be late.
5 I agree to behave responsibility and treat people with respect.
6 I agree not to bring with me, or come to the Project under the influence of drugs or solvents or alcohol.
7 I have read, understood and agree to abide by the Project's Equal Opportunities Policy.
   [Items 6 and 7 were later additions. Earlier contracts included a clause stating that the young person understood he or she might lose his or her place on the Project for breaking the conditions.]

Parent/Guardian

1 I want . . . . to take part in the Junction Project's Intensive Supervision programme. A staff member has explained to me what this is and I understand what will be expected of him/her.
2 I agree to be fully involved in encouraging and helping . . . . to take part in the arrangements for him/her.
3 I agree to attend the contract signing meetings, two reviews and other meetings arranged.
4 I understand that Project staff may be contacting me and

occasionally visiting my home during . . . .'s involvement with them.

5 I understand that I can telephone . . . . whenever I need to and visit the Project by appointment (if possible).

6 I understand that I am invited to attend the Parents' Group, which runs fortnightly.

Professional Worker

1 I want . . . . to take part in the Junction Project's Intensive Supervision programme.

2 I agree to fulfil my part of the agreed programme – see attached.

3 I agree to attend the two reviews and other meetings as arranged by necessity.

4 I understand that it will be my responsibility to take over full supervision of . . . .'s programme at the end of the Junction Project's involvement (for workers holding statutory responsibility). [The reference in item 4 to responsibility after the end of the placement was added after 1984.]

The Junction Project

1 We want . . . . to take part in our Intensive Supervision programme.

2 We agree to meet with . . . . regularly to discuss his/her progress.

3 We agree to liaise with all relevant agencies to monitor the attached programme and inform all parties of its progress.

4 We agree to arrange the two final reviews and other meetings when necessary.

5 We agree to attend court and write reports as appropriate.

The contract is meant to indicate a serious statement of intention by each party. A considerable amount of time is spent explaining obligations to all concerned. If the contract is broken to a significant degree, a review is held. If it is felt the parties still genuinely want to fulfil the terms, specific conditions may be introduced for a set period, about punctuality, for example, or behaviour. In this way the contracts are a starting point for work.

In addition, the parents receive the following letter explaining about the groups for them:

As you know your son/daughter has been given a place at the Junction Project.

Your son/daughter will need your encouragement to help them to make a success of coming to the Junction Project and to stay out of trouble and because of this, we hope you will accept our invitation to come to the Project once a month to meet other parents and to find out what your son/daughter is doing during his/her placement here.

Each evening will deal with a topic which will be relevant to your son/daughter and ourselves and will also have time for a cup of tea and light refreshments.

We would strongly encourage you to attend this 'Parents' Group' because if your son/daughter sees that you are making an effort, it will help them to do the same. This is why we have asked you to sign the Contract.

The group meets from 7.30 p.m. to 9.30 p.m. every last Tuesday of the month. There will always be two members of project staff available to talk to. We will, if you wish, provide transport in the project Minibus.

We are looking forward to meeting you at the Project.

Yours sincerely

Project Leader

Methods of work

The methods of work in the early years and thereafter stemmed from the Project's perspective on delinquency. The November 1982 Interim Report explains:

> The Junction Project recognises that there is a strong link between social and economic deprivation and juvenile delinquency. As such we would not look to explanations based on notions of individual pathology as our starting point in working with young offenders. Nevertheless, the question must be asked why, given similar circumstances certain youngsters become involved in serious delinquent

activity and others do not. To begin to answer this question a variety of factors must be considered including such things as peer group pressure, status and economic frustration, family and particular local circumstances and the operation of the juvenile justice system itself which responds to young offenders in an individual and sometimes arbitrary fashion.

The Project's working approach therefore is to avoid broad generalization and encourage each youngster to identify the salient factors leading to delinquency in his/her case and construct a programme setting targets for effecting change in these areas. In essence, the Project can be regarded as encouraging youngsters to develop their own survival kits for living in the inner city which specifically relate to their own particular circumstances and tackle specific problems. . . .

In anticipating the obvious question 'can the Junction Project stop delinquency?' the Interim Report is succinct: 'The short answer to this must be no'. It goes on to say, however, that the Project does expect, with the majority of youngsters, to have an impact on patterns of offending in terms of both frequency and seriousness.

The methods used with the young people to consider their delinquent behaviour included both groupwork and individual counselling. Although groupwork has remained an important component in the programmes, the Project gradually shifted its balance towards more work on an individual basis. This was partly to meet the needs of individuals better and partly because it was difficult to control the groups and overcome subversive opposition. Materials cited in the 1982 Interim Report which the Project used to enhance life and social skills included *Social Skills and Personal Problem Solving* by Priestley, McGuire, Flegg, Hemsley and Welham (Tavistock, 1978). They liked the approach of self-assessment, setting targets and achieving goals, the variety of exercises, games, quizzes and attractive ploys to engage the interest of young people.

Another important feature of the Project was the involvement of two teachers. The educational package for each young person had to be individually tailored for the obvious reason that abilities and attainments varied greatly, depending often on the amount of time the young person had spent in school. Attendance at school had frequently been reduced by truancy or exclusion. Many of the young people had difficulty with reading and basic number work which it was considered could be

71

addressed by intensive work, even if the period at the Project was short. The Project report *The First Four Years* published in January 1985 states that 'the service provided has in effect been an off-site education unit'.

The Project also gave opportunities to acquire or improve other skills, and hence to foster a sense of individual achievement, by employing sessional workers, for example for guitar lessons, woodwork, photography and mural painting. In addition the Project workers organized sport and visits to places of interest. Each group at the outset had a residential period away from the Project, at centres like Save the Children Fund's 'Hilltop' in Ilkley.

By the time of the 1982 Interim Report, the staff were working in two teams under the Director and Deputy Director. Each team consisted of a leader, a teacher, a project worker, a Community Service Volunteer or student, sessional workers and volunteers, with a shared secretary/ administrator and part-time domestic help. Although the teachers were in charge of the individual education packages, they were also involved in general sessions, and demarcation lines between responsibilities were generally flexible. The Project built in regular supervision by each worker's line manager and in the first three years the staff group met an outside consultant each week for an hour and a half, 'to express issues of an interpersonal nature arising from the pressures of day to day work'. There was also a weekly staff meeting and a training budget to enable staff to go on courses. The weekly staff meeting was central to the success of the Project as it enabled staff to examine their own work and that of their colleagues in a constructive and supportive way, to share problems and to learn from each other. In addition, every 12 to 18 months a review was held at a residential setting outside London, at which all staff considered the overall performance of the Project.

The young people

By 1984 the Project's target group was still young people from Lambeth (or the responsibility of Lambeth), over 12 years old, and about to appear in court for offences likely to attract a custodial sentence. A few limitations had been set from the beginning. The young person had to have stable accommodation within daily travelling distance of the Project, be prepared to sign a contract and not be 'in need of highly specialized help which we could not provide'. Nor was expulsion from the Project ruled out if the young person refused to adhere to the terms of a contract or negotiate a suitable new contract. Given the number of serious offences committed by those before Lambeth courts, such restrictions were practical. It would not be fair on this basis to call the Project selective or to say it had weakened its potential as an alternative to custody for serious offenders, even if it did not have the ever-open door of Dr Barnardo's first institution.

By the end of 1984, 114 young people had started placements, attending full-time for three months and with an individual follow-up programme for a further three months. There are no records available of the characteristics and histories of all of these young people but Maureen Stone, in the report published by the University of Surrey, studied 70 in detail between October 1981 and December 1983. Of these, ten were aged 13, 22 were 15, 30 were 16, seven were 17 and somehow one was 19. All but three were boys. The difficulty of providing suitable programmes for girls who are serious offenders is compounded by the fact that there are so few of them. Although 85 per cent of the sample were born in the UK, over half the fathers on whom information was available were of Afro-Caribbean origin. The majority of parents were in social classes IV and V of the Registrar General's classifications, or were unemployed. Of the 94 parents on whom there was information, nine were dead. Twenty young people lived with both their parents, 21 with one parent only (four with their father) and 10 were in care, living in a children's home, hostel or with foster parents. Twenty-eight were not on any school roll, six were having home tuition, 11 had attended a special school and not surpringly 64 per cent (45) were said to have educational problems.

The picture gained is of boys from deprived backgrounds, with their education usually dislocated, over half from ethnic minorities, forming slightly more than the proportion of black boys of their age in the population. On average they had two previous court appearances. There was only one first offender and the seriousness of the offence which led him to the Project is not given. Most had been involved in crime since the age of 11 and a few from a younger age. Half of the offences which led to them joining the Project were against property and 27 per cent were offences against the person. Maureen Stone concludes that with only two exceptions the young people fitted the selection criteria for the target group.

The study evaluated the project in a number of different ways. It confirmed that about half of the young people did re-offend, although not necessarily in the same way or as seriously as before. This was better than the national rate for re-offending after custody. The researcher also questioned the young people, their parents, the staff and their supervising officers about their perceptions of the Project. The young people were clear about what was being offered by the Project. They saw its main role as being to help them stop offending. They were, however, divided about whether the Project was a punishment or not. They preferred definite rules with sanctions for breaking them and were sceptical about 'talk, talk, that's all you can do. . . .' Their confusion about the welfare element of the Project reflected that of the staff who were concerned about the balance between their roles as representatives of authority and purveyors of welfare. The young people liked the staff and seemed to appreciate what the staff were trying to do, but they identified jobs and money as the key factors which would determine whether they re-offended. Their parents and supervising officers agreed that the Project might have an impact on them as individuals but would not necessarily stop most of them from offending.

The report made various constructive recommendations to clarify referral procedures, ensure that supervising officers were fully conversant with the Project's programmes, systematize report writing and recording, and involve supervising officers and schools more. Only two aspects of the work of the Project were seriously questioned. The first was the extent of the involvement with parents. Did the groups for parents give staff one extra responsibility too much, and was the intrusion into the family fair? Secondly, the place of education in the Project needed to be clarified, including the position regarding those still of school age. The study included a telling case history of the difficulties caused by an incident ending in violence but did not recommend any ways staff could tackle better the problem of handling young people with low levels of self-control who might erupt into violence. Although the racial composition of the young people attending the Project was documented, the fact that the Project had at least one black member of staff was not noted and there were no recommendations about ways the Project could meet any special needs of black young people or the few girls who attended. Finally, the study showed that 27 per cent of young people before the courts who could have been sent to the Project in the period of the research (32 of 118) were not given such an opportunity and received custodial sentences.

Public relations

In its first four years the Project was featured in six television programmes. Its opening had been included on the midday television news, Channel Four had covered it twice and ITV and BBC on their *Help* and *Pebble Mill* programmes. The Director, Martin Farrell, used his skills in communicating to publicize what it was doing not only through the media but also with the local magistrates. Regular invitations were given to magistrates to visit the Project.

The regularity of contact was particularly important in a London borough since the pool of magistrates likely to adjudicate on Lambeth cases was large. It is the Lord Chancellor who appoints magistrates to serve on the Inner London Juvenile Panel. Elsewhere in the country they are elected by their colleagues to serve on the local juvenile panel for a period. The Lord Chancellor also appoints those who are to take the chair in Inner London juvenile courts. This means that to a large extent Inner London juvenile court magistrates are specialists in juvenile offending, although some of them also sit as magistrates in the adult courts. They are appointed to sit in any of the 12 boroughs of Inner London. The same bench of three magistrates sits weekly in each court for three months at a time (a calendar quarter of the year) in order to give continuity to cases where possible. The chairmen stay for five years in the same borough but their two colleagues may change borough every quarter to gain experience of different areas. The task of informing all who may sit in Lambeth is thus of necessity continuing and endless. A chairman is only one among three when it comes to deciding disposals, so it is of first importance for all on the bench to understand the nature of the alternatives available.

The Inner London Juvenile Courts Panel has a Bulletin, published five times a year, which carries articles and book reviews as well as information. There are often contributions about Intermediate Treatment projects in Inner London by magistrates who have visited them or by workers at the projects. In February 1983, the Junction Project was asked if any of the young people would like to write about their experiences in court. Here are two contributions and a picture of the scene headed 'Prehistoric Jury'.

It was the second time I got into trouble that I had to go to Court. The worst part is when you are waiting for your turn, it seems to take years. When it was my turn I went in with my mum behind me. It looked so strange and deserted. I had to stand in front of three ugly-looking people and the one in the middle had glasses on which made it worse because he kept looking at me over the top of them. As the case began he told me to stand and asked me a load of stupid questions. But for some reason I couldn't get the words out of my mouth, it felt as if I was

PREHISTORIC JURY

swallowing big stones, and they were all looking at me, I wanted to run out. Then I answered his questions and he told me to sit down and asked if there were any reports. So a man handed some copies of the reports to the judges sitting at the front and one to me, but I could not be bothered to read it. After they read it the two sitting besides him started to whisper things to him and then he told me to stand and he said that we are going to put you on a year unconditional discharge and he told me what that means and I don't ever want to see you again. As I walked out I was well pleased and I thought to myself that I will never go to court again, but I was back and got away with that one with a fine. But I'm back with the same offence and went to court and they said that I could go away, but they couldn't send me because I wasn't represented by a solicitor and I have to go back in two weeks.

[The Court must have been considering a custodial sentence, thus necessitating a lawyer to represent the young person under the Criminal Justice Act 1982.]

I am 17 years of age. I have attended court around nine times. The offences are all different, shoplifting, stealing by finding etc. The majority of times I have been to court I always feel shaky and scared. I usually pray to God the night before.

Once I went to court charged with shoplifting (theft) with someone else. It wasn't me who was caught with the goods, it was my friend. I did not know she was taking things for I was in another department. Anyway at the end of the case I was fined £42. To me the magistrates were unfair for it was not me that did the actual offence. The magistrate said to me that if I was here again – Borstal straight away.

The last time I attended court was not long ago – in Bromley again. This time I felt bad, bad, bad. The offence was for forgery. I was so scared because I had remembered what the last magistrate had said. Anyway when I was in the box, I looked straight ahead at the magistrate, trying to guess what kind he was. I kept on saying in my head 'Please Lord, forgive me and give me a chance'. Anyway the magistrate listened to my case – and my solicitor suggested for me to attend a scheme in Waterloo. I thought it was a good idea. When the magistrate came up with his decision, he said, 'Will you attend this scheme and keep out of trouble?' I quickly said, 'Yes Sir'. I did mean what I had said. But I didn't believe that the magistrate was going to let me attend the scheme. I was so relieved. The magistrate was very nice and reasonable.

There are times when you are treated fairly and other times when you are treated bad.

But on the whole I have been treated more fairly than badly.

By publishing these accounts the Junction Project and the Bulletin showed how difficult and important it is for juvenile courts to communicate effectively with young people.

Change of management

The Junction Project entered 1985 with a change of control. The voluntary agency, Save The Children Fund, had completed its pump-priming role, as had the DHSS. The local authority, the London Borough of Lambeth, had been sufficiently impressed by the Project's work to take on full financial and managerial responsibility for it. The Project was prestigious enough for any local authority to be proud to run but it took over a year for negotiations about the transfer to be completed.

As far as day-to-day work was concerned the change at first made little difference. The personnel were the same, notably the Director, Martin Farrell, who had shaped it from the beginning. The new Line Manager for the Project in Lambeth Social Services was Julian Holder who, since March 1982, had been a member of the Project's 'Operations Group', which made or ratified all major decisions relating to the policy or practice of the Project. The teachers became responsible to the Inner London Education Authority, a change with some potential difficulties. For example, ILEA teachers had different entitlement to holiday.

However, the implications of joining a bigger, more bureaucratic structure soon emerged. The old steering committee, which fulfilled an advisory and consultative role, had included representatives from the sponsoring bodies (Save the Children Fund, the DHSS, the London Borough of Lambeth and the Cecily Northcote Trust), from the ILEA, the Inner London Probation and Aftercare Service, the London Boroughs' Regional Planning Committee, Lambeth Youth Office, the Metropolitan Police, Lambeth Council for Community Relations, the Commission for Racial Equality, St Thomas's Residents' Association and the Lambeth Juvenile Court. This was the mix of expertise and interest that the DHSS was to recommend for projects under its 1983 initiative.

In the *Report on The First Four Years* published in January 1985, Martin Farrell summed up the advantages of management by a voluntary organization. Apart from access to national networks to influence policy and to raise funds, he wrote 'we have enjoyed a flexibility and immediacy of response which one assumes cannot, with the best will in the world, be offered by a large local Government bureaucracy like Lambeth; we have maintained our own bank account and have very considerable freedom to spend within budget; we have been able to advertise immediately to replace staff, or to appoint locum workers at short notice, and have thereby not had any post vacant for more than a month; access to and by the media has been more straightforward than one assumes it would be under local authority management'.

These words, especially about staff recruitment, were to prove prescient when Farrell himself left in September 1986 to become General Secretary of the Institute for the Study and Treatment of Delinquency (ISTD). Although he gave several months' notice of his departure, the new Project Director, Valerie Jones, was not appointed until August 1987. The reason for the delay in this and other appointments was due to what have been described as Lambeth's 'Byzantine' selection procedures. During this period, in addition to an equal opportunities policy shared by many London boroughs and particularly appropriate to a project like the Junction, Lambeth gave priority for jobs to disabled people and long procedures had to be followed before a vacancy could be offered to an able-bodied person. As a result of depleted staffing, only 30 young people attended the Project in 1986 and in August 1987 there were only six currently following programmes. Once these temporary doldrums were passed, the Project looked set to continue vigorous work but the perils of the transition show how quickly a project, even if well-established, can lose momentum.

New features

Although the target group of the Project remained the same – serious offenders in danger of custody – some of its methods changed after a review of the Project's work in the spring of 1986. The system of contracts was still central but young people now had individual programmes, drawn up after assessment of their needs and the seriousness and nature of their offence. The duration of a placement varied from two to six months or occasionally was longer. Full-time attendance was required from some young people and the minimum attendance was two sessions a week. Any programme could include a measure of reparation to the victim, following the development of a reparation scheme from 1985.

An important change was that the Project usually asked the court for a Supervision Order with requirements for specified activities as the legal basis for placement instead of a deferred sentence. The two staff teams became 'the gatekeeping team' and 'the programme team'. The gate-keepers became responsible for identifying appropriate referrals, assessing referrals, writing reports for courts, appearing in courts, liaising with other agencies over referrals and appeals, and monitoring the outcomes at court. They also were to develop provision for Lambeth juveniles given custodial sentences.

Young people became the responsibility of the programmes team once attendance was agreed by the court. As well as drawing up the contracts, providing a key worker for each participant, running the programmes, writing any further court reports, and calling reviews, this team liaised with parents and other agencies. The timetable included programmes from 9.30 a.m. to 8.00 p.m. on Mondays, Tuesdays and Thursdays, with Wednesdays and Fridays half days. The evening sessions were planned for those in full-time education or work but an educational programme was still available during the day for others.

In a document consulting magistrates and social workers about the new arrangements, Valerie Jones explained that the Project offered alternatives to all Custodial Orders, from short Detention Centre Orders to Section 53 sentences imposed by the Crown Court. The new system was based on there being two full-time and one part-time member of the gatekeeping team and five members of the programmes team, including two teachers, plus a Project Leader and Deputy Leader. As part of the move towards individual programmes the Project planned to develop specialized offending programmes to address specific types of offence. 'Our concern at the moment', she said, 'is with offences involving violence as many young people are receiving custody for offences of Grievous Bodily Harm, Actual Bodily Harm and Robbery, for which alternatives are not being considered.'

So by 1987 what kind of young people were the Junction Project aiming to work with? Here is a report submitted to the court, with identifying details changed:

Pete (aged 16) first became known to the Junction Project 18 months ago. He was sent here following convictions for theft from motor vehicles to attend on a twice-weekly basis whilst on a deferment of sentence. He had an extremely successful placement which was reflected when he returned to court three months later and received conditional discharges on all three matters.

Whilst attending the Project Pete was noted by staff for his compliant and quiet manner. He completed all the work set for him without disagreement or bother of any sort. He always did as he was asked, was quite shy, sometimes nervous or anxious and was certainly not the sort of youngster who sought attention and status by the way of disruptive, violent or intimidating behaviour – quite the opposite in fact. Our only fears for Pete were that he was exactly the sort of young person who would be 'picked on' by a more aggressive type looking for an 'easy' victim to bully. Pete at that time was small for his age and very slight in build. It was therefore with considerable surprise that we learned that he was appearing before this court for an offence of violence as this information certainly did not tie in with the personality that we had known 12 months previously.

Following Pete's appearance before this court a month ago when the Court indicated very strongly that a custodial sentence was being considered, I contacted the Probation Officer preparing reports and have spoken with Pete about the offence. Unfortunately, I have been unable to speak directly with Pete's solicitor to confirm whether Pete's view of the offence and its causes is accepted.

I am informed by Pete and the Probation Officer that the offence occurred after the victim had spent some six weeks at the Youth Training Scheme where Pete was taunted and treated with some degree of derision by the victim including very hurtful comments being made about Pete's parents. That Pete had told him to stop but that this request had been greeted by laughter and an increase of the activity. On the day in question, following a 'good' day when the victim was absent from work, he had returned to work and the taunting began again. Pete approached him and told him to stop, he was laughed at again and in a reaction of uncontrolled anger Pete 'cracked' (his words) and committed the offence. I asked Pete if he had consciously taken the Stanley knife with him when he approached the victim with the intention of using it or threatening to use it. He said that he had not. He was using the knife in his work and had not thought to put it down. Thus, it appears that the offence was committed spontaneously, the result of an outburst of pent-up rage and frustration following weeks of attempted intimidation and misery.

This explanation of what occurred I feel did tie in with the Junction Project's impression of this boy as one who others would attempt to victimize and unfortunately whilst not excusing his action we could see how it could happen. Having established, as far as possible, what were the facts of the case the Junction Project has to consider whether we could offer anything to the Court as an alternative to custodial sentence, given that Pete has already attended the Project before, albeit for offences of a very different nature. We were aware that the Probation Officer had referred Pete for community service assessment and that his employers at the Youth Training Scheme where the incident occurred would be keen to retain him in their scheme as they had been very pleased with his work.

We felt that the only thing that the Junction Project could offer the Court that would be appropriate to this case would be a specific, tailor-made programme which focussed on the offence, Pete's aggressive and unlawful response to provocation, with the aims of making clear the effects, short and long term, of such action, and the exploitation of strategies to avoid such responses in future. The details of this programme have been worked out and are attached. It is designed to take place over 12 weekly sessions of two hours. If it were to take place in the evenings it would allow Pete to maintain his progress on his Youth Training Scheme.

Conclusion

We are aware that the court must be considering imposing a custodial sentence and we are mindful of the abhorrence with which it views offences involving violence. However, we would urge the Court to consider that custody in this case is neither necessary nor inevitable.

The act of cutting someone with a knife so that 11 stitches are required is serious. However, given the specific circumstances of this offence – the taunting, the build up of feelings within Pete and the spontaneous nature of the offence – we would argue that a non-custodial sentence, as long as it is firm enough, would be acceptable to a general member of the public who is informed of the full facts of the case.

Pete is not, by nature, a violent, malicious or aggressive person. He committed the offence under provocation and immediately recognized and regretted that his retaliation was too severe. The evidence of his character would indicate that he is not a danger to the general public. It is questionable whether custody would serve as a deterrent as it would not necessarily prevent a re-occurrence in a similar situation. What is required, we believe, is planned work to be done on changing behaviour. The programme offered by the Junction Project goes some way towards achieving this aim. We feel that it is unlikely that such work can be done in the environment of a Detention Centre or Youth Custody Centre.

Finally, Pete has responded positively to community disposals in the past. During the period of time he attended the Junction Project he was observed to mature over the three months and it was felt that he was one of those who would 'grow out' of crime. Until this new and very different sort of offence he had not committed an offence since the one that originally brought him to the Project. When I described the sort of programme that the Junction Project were considering for him he expressed positive interest and agreed he would co-operate. He was also positive in his view of community service and given his attendance record at the Junction Project I have no doubts that he would fulfil such an order if it were imposed.

Recommendation

We are aware that if the Court were prepared to consider a non-custodial disposal then the programme proposed by the Junction Project may not on its own satisfy the Court in terms of its adequacy as a firm punishment. Therefore, although we considered recommending a Supervision Order with a Specified Activity Requirement we felt that this may not satisfy the Bench. A deferred sentence of three months may be the most appropriate course of action as it allows the Bench to follow the progress of the programme and consider a suitable sentence at the end of deferment in the light of the work done.

Alternatively, the Court may choose to follow a recommendation of a Community Service Order. As we have already indicated, our knowledge of Pete leads us to support the view that he would complete such an order and apply himself constructively to it. If the Court wished to follow this course of action then the Junction Project, unusually, would be prepared to work with Pete in our programme in a voluntary capacity. Pete feels that he has sufficient interest in what he offers to motivate himself to attend. However, I would emphasize that as co-operation would be voluntary then the status of the Junction Project programme as an alternative to custody would not exist and its completion would depend entirely on Pete's motivation. There will be a member of staff from the Junction Project in Court should any further information be required.

Proposed Junction Project Programme for Pete

This programme has been developed with the full co-operation of Pete, his mother and the Probation Officer in the case. The aim of this programme is to enable Pete to develop personal strategies that will allow him to respond appropriately to stress and provocation. It aims to make clear the unacceptability of aggressive and violent behaviour. The overall objective of this programme is to effect a behavioural change in Pete that will reduce the likelihood, if not ensure, that Pete does not commit a similar offence in future.

Part One – Self Awareness Three weekly sessions of two hours each based on written work and discussions using materials produced in the field of 'Social and Personal Education'. These sessions will be run by an experienced, qualified teacher and social worker.

Part Two – Offence Programme Six further weekly sessions of two hours each, again involving written work and discussion. In addition Pete will be expected to complete Art and Drama work. The focus of all these sessions will be the offence heard today. The materials which will be used in these sessions have been produced in the field of 'Social and Personal Education' and by the University of Lancaster. These sessions will be run by a qualified and experienced teacher and an experienced Youth Worker and IT worker.

Part Three – Assertiveness Training Three further weekly sessions of two hours each involving written work and discussion. They will focus on the importance of behaving assertively and non-violently. Again the material to be used has been developed in the field of 'Social and Personal Education'. These sessions will be run by an experienced teacher and social worker.

Pete received a three-week Detention Centre Order. He is an example of a boy for whom the Project failed to win a second chance. Lawrence, a 16 year-old who had committed a number of serious burglaries but who had not attended the Project before, was given a deferred sentence for six months to attend the Project. A long report explaining the assessment of Lawrence over six appointments concluded as follows:

During the course of the assessment Lawrence has identified three goals he would like to achieve if the court allows him to attend the Junction Project. These are:
1 Not to re-offend.
2 To improve his handwriting
3 To begin to learn a trade either through an apprenticeship or a Youth Training Scheme.
To enable Lawrence to achieve these goals the Junction Project is able to offer him a placement that will last six months. Initially,

Lawrence will be expected to attend the Project on Mondays, Tuesdays and Thursdays. However, once Lawrence gains a place at a Youth Training Scheme, a job or a college placement, his attendance at the Project will be reduced to allow him to pursue his career/training.

During his placement Lawrence would be expected to:

1 *Engage in Law and Offending Work* The aim of this work is to confront Lawrence with the consequences of his behaviour and to enable him to continue in his resolve not to re-offend.

2 *Education* The aim of this work is to ensure that Lawrence has sufficient educational skills to enable him to follow his chosen career (a skill in the building trade) and to improve his writing to a standard of which he can be proud.

3 *Social Skills and Career Guidance* (In co-operation with Brixton Careers Service.) The aim of this is to enable Lawrence to follow through his desire to learn a 'trade'.

4 *Options* Lawrence has chosen to engage in cookery and basketball. The aim of 'options' is to encourage project members to develop an appropriate leisure-time pursuit.

In conclusion to this lengthy report I would like to inform the Magistrates that I believe that, with the support of his parents, Lawrence has both the ability and commitment to respond constructively to a community alternative to custody. Whilst recognising the seriousness of the offences being heard today I believe that Lawrence has already received a 'painful' form of punishment, i.e. he has seen how upset he has made his parents and is remorseful for this and he has had his liberty restricted by his parents. At this stage I think that custody would serve only to confirm Lawrence's feelings of lack of purpose by separating him from supportive parents and forcing him to live with young men many of whom will have entrenched criminal attitudes.

Of the nine young people attending the Project in the summer of 1987, four had committed burglaries, four offences involving violence (assault or robbery) and one theft and criminal damage. There was only one young person in Maureen Stone's sample of 70 between October 1981 and December 1983 who had no previous offences before attending the Project. However, four of the nine at this period had not been before the courts before. One, a white boy, had committed six burglaries of domestic properties. Nothing had been recovered of the goods he had stolen which were worth several thousand pounds. The second, a black boy who was in care on a voluntary basis and had been suspended from his school, had committed robbery and been found in possession of an offensive weapon. The third, again black but in full-time employment, had been convicted of robbery and two offences of possession of offensive weapons. The fourth, a black boy who did not attend school but who had gone to an Intermediate Treatment group on a voluntary basis, had committed a burglary. It seems that the courts had been considering custody for these first offenders because of the seriousness of their offences and thus they met the Project's selection criteria.

An important consequence for the Project of young people attending under Supervision Orders with requirements for specified activities, was a definite procedure if a young person breached an order. Previously workers had been unable to return young people on deferred sentences to the courts for non-attendance or breaking Project rules. In a paper for a consultation meeting with magistrates and social workers about the new arrangements in February 1987, the Project explained: 'It allows us to return the young person to court should he/she breach the order. The court can then deal with the young person regarding the breach and the status of the Junction Project as an alternative to custody sentence is reinforced. It avoids the issue of "double sentencing" where, frequently, after a long and successful hard worked period of deferment the young person returns to court to receive another (in their eyes) sentence on top of what they have already completed.'

The procedure about breaches was included in the contracts signed by all the parties. The young person's contract stated: 'I understand that if I do not attend the Junction Project I will be returned to court by the Project and my social worker. The arrangements for doing this have been explained to me.' The arrangements were detailed. A medical certificate was required for any absence because of illness. On the first unverified absence a standard letter would be sent first class or delivered by hand with copies to the social worker. It restated the attendance requirements and the consequences of any future absences. On the second absence the young person would be visited at home on the same day or the day after the missed appointment and a letter left for him or her, whether or not the worker had found them at home. If the young person did not attend the next appointment at the Project, an emergency review would be held within five working days. If the young person began attending again before the review, the contract could be re-negotiated. If the young person agreed at the review to attend again, breach proceedings would be started for a date four weeks ahead which could be cancelled if all went well. If the young person did not attend the review, breach proceedings would go ahead after every effort had been made to contact the young person. Under the new arrangements the Project specified in its original report to the court the starting date of the specified activities and subsequent dates for attendance, including an open clause to enable any short residential component.

An important advantage of the Project being in the mainstream of Lambeth's provision for Intermediate Treatment, under the same management as the other projects, was its formal integration in the Borough's planning for children and young people. The IT Section, with two IT officers to supervise all the projects, was with the Courts Section and the Section for Children in Care, part of the Adolescent and Children's Division of the Personal Social Services Department. There was a monthly meeting for the managers of all the statutory projects. Links were still maintained with the voluntary sector through an IT Group which had representatives from those working in both sectors. The loss caused by the change of management, however, was in the links with other agencies at management level which had been built into the former management structure. Nor was there any direct contact with elected members of the Council.

Does a change to local authority management guarantee stability? In theory it should. That is why a condition of pump-priming under the DHSS 1983 initiative was that the Project should eventually be integrated into the area's permanent provision. But local authorities like other organizations are subject to shifts in policy and, especially in the late 1980s, to pressure on their resources. In 1988 Lambeth had to cut £62m from its services to balance its budget. It axed 1,000 jobs, including one and a half social worker posts and half an administrative post at the Junction Project. In addition, one of the ILEA teacher posts was frozen, leaving the Project with a smaller staff than when it started.

Mediation, reparation and conciliation

The Project has had no regular involvement in the community comparable with the pre-employment, community service and accommodation schemes developed by the Juvenile Offender Resource Centre in Surrey but from 1985 it has pioneered a programme for improving relations between young offenders and their victims. The scheme was originally intended for young people who re-offended whilst at the Project, but in

1986 it was decided to extend it, when there were sufficient staff, to be part of the ordinary programmes offered by the Project on social skills, the law and offending. The central idea was to bring together the parties, if both agreed, for a discussion. Afterwards the young person might do some useful tasks for the victim, perhaps repairing any damage, or, if the victim preferred, do some voluntary work instead for the community, but the most important part was the meeting between them.

In keeping with the Project's policy of informing and consulting magistrates, the progress of the scheme was explained at one of the local Benches' training meetings in March 1987. Two videos were shown, one in which the former Director of the Project, Martin Farrell, was interviewed about the scheme by Magnus Magnusson on *Pebble Mill at One*, and one made by the National Intermediate Treatment Federation (NITFed) for training new workers in the field. The procedure followed is that the key worker first of all discusses the idea with the young person. If the young person wishes to proceed, the key worker contacts the police and local victim support organization. The police contact the victim. If the victim does not wish to proceed, the matter rests there. If the victim is interested, a representative from the victim support organization visits and gives further information. If the victim then agrees to proceed a mediation session is arranged.

The mediation sessions are always held in the presence of an independent third party, the mediator, whose role is crucial. The process of mediation aims to bring about conciliation between the victim and the offender and it is stressed that this may or may not lead to reparation. During the conciliation process 'the offender grows aware of the effect s/he has had on the victim and thus "feels" for the victim. Likewise the victim is able to share the experience of the offender and thus s/he feels less vulnerable and less singled out. To bring about conciliation the process of mediation has to be carefully planned and sensitively handled.'

Although at first sight mediation schemes might be thought to offer the victim nothing but additional strain, growing evidence from their use suggests that victims find positive benefits. The most usual is that the young person who entered their house and stole their belongings or who damaged their property is less frightening to meet than to imagine. Most victims imagine or remember their attackers as bigger, tougher and more powerful than they often are, so it can be a relief to see them at a controlled meeting. Offenders also have fantasies about their victims, although some do not think about them at all. It is much more effective for them to hear from the actual victim the harm they have done them than to have it explained in abstract by someone else. The encounter makes it real and enables them to begin to see themselves in the victim's place. To apply one theory of moral education, people have to have knowledge of the implications of their actions in order to make the right choices but they also have to have sufficient emotional involvement to see the relevance of the knowledge and to want to act. A face-to-face encounter with a victim can give an offender the emotional insight that is needed.

The Project workers quote as a good example the first case undertaken through the scheme in 1984. The young offender had stolen, and damaged badly while he drove it, a car which was the hobby and pride of its owner. The owner had spent all his spare time improving and maintaining the car. He was very angry at the outset of the interview, shouting at the offender that it was no good making excuses about what a hard life he had since he had had just as hard a life. He had been brought up in care but had built himself a successful life in which the car was part of a dream come true. The effect on the offender was electric to meet someone who had experienced the same upbringing as himself, who knew what it was to long for a car as the key to a different world. After two and a half hours they were exchanging tales about their experiences in children's homes and at the end of the session they shook hands with more amiability than it had been thought possible.

By the end of 1987 the Project had brought together six victims with their offenders. Although many victims are altruistic enough to want to help young offenders, the number of cases suitable for this work is not large. Moreover the process is time-consuming and therefore costly if undertaken properly. However, as a means to rehabilitate offenders such schemes clearly have potential and at national level there has been growing interest in them. In 1984 a Home Office research paper by Tony Marshall, *Reparation, Conciliation and Mediation* (Research and Planning Unit Paper 27), gave details of the various types of schemes in existence or projected, including the Junction Project's. The DHSS is conducting research into four schemes in Carlisle, Coventry, Leeds and Wolverhampton. Among the questions to be answered are the relative value of direct and indirect reparation – will a young person (like Keith in Surrey) see the point of cleaning a different wall from the one on which he or she scrawled graffiti? Some would prefer such schemes to be used for their intrinsic worth but not by order of the court. And how acceptable would it be with the public for such schemes to be used to divert young people from appearing in court and being punished in the criminal justice system?

Controversial issues

By the end of 1987 the Junction Project was increasing its involvement in the local community. Its geographical situation, nearer the Houses of Parliament than Railton Road, Brixton, had been one reason why at the beginning it was so self-contained, offering full day care on the premises. In addition to a large sitting-room, two interview rooms, an office, an education room and a big, light kitchen with a dining area, there is a sports hall for pool, basket-ball, table tennis, table football and carpentry. The lease on its building expires in 1989 when the area, close to Waterloo station, is scheduled for redevelopment for the channel tunnel terminus. A more central site would make contact with other agencies and access for everyone easier. Meanwhile, links with the community have been strengthened not only through projects like the mediation and reparation scheme. The Project works more closely with local community education schemes, which can offer a young person a longer period of compensatory education, Youth Training Schemes and the Lambeth Community Service Scheme (which is distinct from the community service scheme for offenders organized by the probation service).

The Project has two computers which are used to teach the young people computing and are part of the equipment for the programmes, like the video camera and the music synthesiser. They are not used to gather and monitor statistics about the Project or the Lambeth juvenile justice system. However, in 1987 the Project gathered what statistics it could for 1986, examined them and came to two uncomfortable conclusions. First, the figures indicated that the Project was not being used as an alternative to custody for many offenders whose crimes involved violence. Was this because the courts thought that crimes of this kind necessitated custody, or were they not convinced that the Project offered suitable programmes for such offenders? Secondly, why were twice as many black juveniles as white given custodial sentences in Lambeth, while less than half of those sent to the Project in the year were black? Was there some discrimination operating, conscious, unconscious or institutionalized?

The details collected were of those young people facing the likelihood of custody. Of 52 offenders before the courts whose offences involved violence, only 14, just over a third, received an alternative to custody. Fewer than half of other serious offenders were sent into custody. We have seen that in 1986 Lambeth had a higher proportion of offences involving violence, 18 per cent, than neighbouring boroughs, so violence was clearly a grave local issue, especially since juveniles nationally commit few violent offences.

The figures also showed that 31 of the 38 young people sentenced to custody for crimes involving violence were black, and 11 of the 14 sent to the Project were black, yet the proportion of black young people in the community was not more than 50 per cent.

Here are the awkward questions about the links between violence and race which these figures raised for the Project.

It is clear that robbery and crimes of violence are the types of offences most likely to attract a custodial sentence and to gain least sympathy from the courts. It is also clear that a far higher proportion of black youths than white youths were sentenced to custody or received an alternative for offences of robbery and violence (83 per cent of the total for robbery and 76 per cent of the total for violence). We can only speculate as to the reality of what happens on the street but such figures present a very worrying picture . . . the police have targetted street crime in recent years and . . . see black youths as the major perpetrators of such crimes. More black youths are therefore appre-hended for these sorts of offences and we see the results coming through the courts in terms of custodial and alternative to custody sentences. Thus the figures begin to 'justify' the stereotype of the 'black mugger' . . . In educational circles the self-fulfilling prophecy aspect of teacher-pupil expectations has now been accepted . . . a similar process could easily take place in the field of crime . . . and not only the police but IT workers, social workers and other youth workers can contribute to this process.

The involvement of black people in violent crime, especially the kind of frightening bag-snatching that is often called mugging, is a topic that people of liberal views find embarrassing to discuss. As a result it is not often examined dispassionately, which does no one, least of all the black community, any service. It is important first of all to look more closely at the phenomenon of robbery, which in legal terminology is 'stealing and immediately before or at the time of doing so, and in order to do so, using force on any person or putting or seeking to put any person in fear of being then and there subjected to force'. The complicating factor is that the amount of force necessary to change theft into robbery may be assessed differently from area to area and by different police forces making charges. It has been pointed out that Brixton has a high rate of robbery but a comparatively low rate of theft. When the two sets of figures are combined the total is similar to that in many other areas. Is robbery defined more widely than elsewhere? The question is difficult to answer but the consequences of the same crime being labelled differently can be grave for the offender since robbery obviously is treated more severely.

The Project workers point out that in certain areas of Lambeth, being forced to hand over your possessions is a fact of life from the time of entry into local secondary schools. The first year lose their dinner money to the older and stronger. They in turn learn either to pay a little to protect themselves or to rob the next to arrive. Each school deals differently with such offences, most by internal sanctions, a few by involving the police. The salient point is that most local children have themselves been victims and see this kind of robbery as a feature of their everyday lives. It is not excusable but it is not surprising that some of them apply the same tactics out of school – and most of the victims of such violent crimes are not old ladies but people of under 30, generally of similar social background, race and age to their assailants. This description of a culture in which it is normal for the strongest to take the available cash makes greed the motivation: the only way to acquire spending money in this deprived area is to take it from someone else. Such an explanation of the prevalence of street robbery rates moral standards low but is probably more convincing than the political view which sees crime involving violence by black youths as a special form of social protest. In one of the few thoughtful discussions of these issues, John Pitts, a social work lecturer with experience of Intermediate Treatment from its earliest days, reports in his contribution to *Confronting Crime* (edited by Roger Matthews and Jock Young, Sage, 1986), and in *The Politics of Juvenile Crime* (Sage, 1988), how this kind of crime has been seen by some commentators as a mode of resistance to racial oppression and over-zealous policing. Although anyone who knows the black community in Lambeth will testify to the high level of awareness on racial issues and a pervasive sense of the injustice suffered by those who dwell in Babylon, to suggest that street robberies have a conscious political intention does not make sense. It could only be feasible if the attacks were all on white people or even on other ethnic minorities, but they are not. At least half are on other black people, of West Indian as well as Asian origin. Possibly there is more tolerance of this kind of crime because of political disaffection but for every anti-establishment, political activist there can be found a God-fearing West Indian parent, horrified by the sin against the accepted moral code.

The accusation that society and those in the criminal justice system (starting with the police, continuing through the juvenile courts and including the welfare workers) are pre-disposed to associate black youth with violent crime, and therefore find what they are seeking, has more substance but is simplistic. There is certainly a chicken-and-egg logic that stems from looking at statistics about crime by young people. Black young people meet overt racism but they are often also likely to be penalized because white people are not sure how to treat them and because they and their families are unfamiliar with official systems. As they are processed through the system the cards stacked against them grow in number. The trouble can begin at the scene of the crime (many arrests for aggressive behaviour occur after the arrival of the police), continue at the police station and go on through the welfare agencies if white social workers and solicitors do not have rapport with their clients. Lack of confidence in black families through lack of knowledge may subtly influence the alternatives offered in court reports and accepted by the Bench. Confusion about black family life-styles may lead to the view that black young people need punishment and discipline in custody. They may be sent away for seemingly contradictory reasons, either because it is thought that they are allowed to run wild and come from a disorganized background or because it is thought they are used to a strict, authoritarian pattern of child-rearing and so will not respond to measures in the community. It is a complex and slow task to eradicate this kind of subconscious racism and stereotyping but it is a task that must be tackled urgently through public education and above all by training and appointing more black police officers, social workers and magistrates.

The common sense of such policies has been accepted since the Scarman Report of 1981 but progress is slow. Good will alone is not enough. There has to be easier access for people from ethnic minorities to training (which does not mean any diminution of standards at qualification). One way to accelerate progress is by regular ethnic monitoring not only of the various professions but also of offenders. It is neither discriminatory nor accusatory to know the proportion of offenders before the courts who are black. It is a factual matter on which it is vital to be accurate when weighing all the elements to be considered.

It should also be pointed out that if at the moment more black than white young people are found guilty of street robberies, more white than black young people are violent football hooligans, carrying horrendous weapons. Moreover, if the argument is accepted that most of these juvenile robberies are opportunist, then there are ways to divert the young people concerned into other activities. The dearth of attractive but inexpensive facilities for young people's leisure is a topic in itself, as will be discussed in the chapter of this book on youth work in Sunderland.

The second uncomfortable issue raised by the workers at the Junction Project in 1987 was the difficulty of convincing magistrates that it was appropriate to punish offences which involved violence by means other than a spell in custody. The rigour of the alternative is one factor here, as the experience in Surrey, albeit for far fewer cases, has shown. There is also now a need for more courses to be developed which tackle not just offending behaviour but violent behaviour. It is a truism that a spell in custody will punish a young person but do nothing to teach control of feelings, even if it shows the consequences of losing control. In the community there can be training in social skills and practice in avoiding confrontations.

Key features

A deprived area with a high rate of delinquency and serious crime is especially challenging to the talents and dedication of those working with young people at risk. The Junction Project was founded to face this challenge with a staff from different professional backgrounds including teachers. The role of the first Project Leader or Director is always crucial and the Project benefited to the full from Martin Farrell's gifts for explaining and publicizing the Project's work. Here are some key features of the Project over its seven-year duration.

• An early example, which became a model for others, of a project which is an alternative to custody and care, begun by a partnership between central government and local statutory and voluntary agencies.

• Operates in an extremely deprived area.

• Operates in an area with a higher than usual rate of crime involving violence by juveniles.

• Operates in an area with a large West Indian population.

• Operates in an area with large numbers and a high turn-over of social workers, magistrates and others.

• Uses contracts to clarify aims and expectations with all parties.

• Changed its working methods after experience from fixed groups to individual programmes.

• Begun by asking courts to defer sentence on young people while they attended, but asked courts to make Supervision Orders with requirements for specified activities as the legal basis for attendance when that option became available.

● Offered full-time remedial education on site at first.

● Involvement of parents in group meetings.

● Gradual increase of liaison with other agencies in the community.

● Regular meetings with magistrates.

● Innovative mediation and reparation scheme.

● Subject of a research study from October 1981 to December 1983.

● In general, no continuing monitoring of its place or effect in the juvenile justice system.

● Sensitive to special needs of black young people, employing black staff.

● Received national publicity as a pioneering project.

● Affected by change of management and incorporation into a local authority.

4

Including Education
Kirklees Metropolitan District Council

In October 1987 a notice, headed NEW JUVENILE JUSTICE RESOURCES – YOUR CHANCE TO FIND OUT MORE, was circulated throughout Kirklees to all agencies involved with young people. It read as follows.

> In the course of the next few weeks, a full range of resources for work with young offenders throughout Kirkless will become operational. These resources, and the overall strategy which they underpin, have the backing of all the main statutory agencies which work with young offenders – Social Services, Probation Service and Education Social Work Service.
>
> In order to inform you about what the resources will offer and how places on them are obtained, a series of open meetings has been arranged to which interested parties from all agencies are invited. You are invited to attend whichever meeting is most convenient for you . . . so that information is widely shared and the resources are used to the full.

Dates and different times of day were given for meetings at six places in Kirklees, the Yorkshire metropolitan district which includes Huddersfield, Dewsbury, Batley and the Spen Valley.

The new, unified provision for young offenders throughout Kirklees had evolved in the wake of KEY (Kirklees Enterprise for Youth) set up in response to the DHSS Circular LAC/83. KEY's first unusual feature was that it consisted of three separate but complementary projects, each staffed and run by a different voluntary agency but under a manager employed by the Social Services Department and seconded to KEY. The three voluntary agencies involved were Barnardo's, the Children's Society and the National Children's Centre. From the start all the main statutory agencies in Kirklees were involved (social services, probation, education and the police) as were the Juvenile Bench and the regional DHSS Social Work Service. The final report on KEY's three years of existence explains 'This collaborative approach was vital to the achievement of KEY's objectives and served to emphasize that the young people with whom the KEY projects worked were ultimately the responsibility of all the agencies in Kirklees and that a combined approach was necessary in order to serve their needs effectively.'

The KEY projects were thus grounded in the general provision of the area for young people, with social services from the outset contributing one third of the costs, although their focus under the DHSS initiative was to provide alternatives to custody and care. They consciously planned to foster a multi-disciplinary approach to the problems of young people who had reached a point of crisis through offending.

Some elements were common to the three projects. The criteria for acceptance to them all were that the young people were likely to receive a custodial sentence, had some kind of home-base in Kirklees (which could include residential care) and agreed to attend if the court so ordered. There were no restrictions on the seriousness of the offence or the previous record of the offender. There was no limitation on numbers. The service would always be made available even if more young people had to be accepted than the project had originally envisaged. Work began on the day of the court's disposal and the projects had continuous, 'rolling' programmes into which new members could be slotted as they arrived. The work to be undertaken was described in detail in court and to the young people, parents and supervising officers before they joined. The young people, parents and project workers signed contracts at the start. There was a clear policy about the consequences of breaching the conditions of the orders. Young people who failed to co-operate with their projects were returned to the court but this was not used as a means to remove them from the project.

Children's Society Tracking Project

The most intensive of the three projects was the Children's Society Tracking Project. Tracking as a penal term originated in the US to describe schemes through which offenders lived in the community but were under constant surveillance and had to contact their supervisors every day, if not more often. The concept of tracking has met vigorous opposition in the UK, particularly from the National Association of Probation Officers, as being a draconian restriction of liberty, unlikely in itself to change behaviour or nurture a sense of personal responsibility, and intruding unacceptably into the lives of offenders' families. It has been particularly opposed when used during a period of assessment when the juvenile is on bail and when untrained volunteers have maintained the contacts. A NAPO policy document on juvenile offenders, issued in 1986 (PD 2/86), explains that 'the main concern with policing runs contrary to the social work development which we have sought to encourage in work with juvenile offenders, it threatens civil liberties and is a clear abuse of the intentions of the Bail Act'. In Kirklees, however, there was no opposition to the introduction of tracking, possibly because it was presented from the start as part of an integrated programme for the young people. It was seen as merely one aspect of intensive supervision.

The target group for this project was 14 to 17 year-olds who would otherwise be sentenced to a long custodial sentence of three months or more. They were the most serious and persistent offenders, some of whom had previously been in custody, especially detention centres, or had formerly attended Intermediate Treatment projects. In 1983, the year before KEY opened its doors, the three juvenile courts of Kirklees sent into custody 118 young people, 21 per cent of 14 to 16 year-old males who appeared before them, (28 per cent at Batley, 18 per cent at Dewsbury and 18 per cent at Huddersfield). The national average was 12 per cent. Whatever the reasons, a great many young people in the area were being sent into custody so there was clearly scope for a project which could convince the courts that it had a rigorous alternative to offer.

The staff consisted of a project leader, Barbara Martin, five part-time trackers, two part-time group workers and one part-time clerical and administrative officer. The project used two methods of work, individual supervision and counselling by the tracker, and work in groups. Initially the young person met the tracker assigned every day. In addition the tracker might check the young person's whereabouts or contact him or her by telephone at different times during the day. Tracking continued for the four months the young person attended the project but the frequency of contact gradually decreased. The tracker throughout aimed to help the young person organize his or her time in a constructive way and to provide intensive support and practical advice in relation to family, home, school, work and finances. The tracker encouraged the young person to use the conventional facilities within the community, liaising with schools regularly, for example, and offered continuing contact as necessary at the end of the compulsory period.

The groups met on two evenings each week with a programme that ran for three months. Each young person could enter the group after a brief personal induction as soon as the court made the disposal, since the topics covered were separate modules including aspects of offending and the law, social skills, self awareness, employment or unemployment and personal relationships.

The project explained these features to magistrates in a two-page document which also set out the legal basis on which it suggested a young person should be placed. Initially it asked for the young person to be remanded on conditional bail for 28 days in order that his or her response to the project could be assessed. If there was a satisfactory level of co-operation from the young person, a Supervision Order for one year was requested with a specified activities clause under Section 12(3)c of the Children and Young Persons Act 1969. 'The KEY Children's Society Project', the document claimed, 'provides courts in Kirklees with a comprehensive and direct alternative to custody sentences of three months and above. It provides immediate, intensive and flexible supervision and advice, and embodies both care and control. It is directed towards the young person acquiring the skills and structure necessary to live in society without recourse to offending.' The document ended by promising that the court would be informed if the young person failed to co-operate.

In addition, magistrates were informed of the contracts to be agreed by the young person, the parents and the project. Overleaf is a young person's contract for the bail period.

---

1. I understand that as a result of the offences I have committed, I could have been sent to a Youth Custody Centre or a Detention Centre when I appeared in Court on . . . Instead I have agreed to participate in the KEY scheme and have the conditions explained to me.

2. I agree that it is my responsiblity to stay out of trouble and that I will co-operate with the Project Staff in doing this by:

   a) Keeping all appointments and arrangements made with the Tracker.
   b) Keeping the Tracker informed of my movements and discussing any problems I may have.
   c) Participating actively in the sessions. I agree specifically to permit video recordings of some activity to be made.

3. It has been explained to me that if I do not comply with the instructions that I receive from the Project Staff that I would be breaking the agreement that I have made with the Project and the Court and that this will mean that I will have to go back to Court and that it could result in my being sent to Youth Custody or Detention Centre.

4. *Missed Appointment* If I do not contact the Project within two hours of missing my appointment, the Police will be informed with a view to my being arrested and returned before the Court.

My Trackers's name is ....

Phone No. ....

Signed ....

The distinctive feature of this contract is the way it spells out clearly first that the project really is an alternative to custody and second that custody may be the penalty for not co-operating.

As at other projects which use contracts, the reciprocal nature of the agreement is stressed by a short declaration from the tracker:

I accept that my job is to help . . . . stay out of trouble. I will take a personal interest in him/her and help him/her to learn about and do things that will help him/her to avoid further Court appearances. I will ensure that . . . . is aware of the regulations governing his/her access to Project records and that he/she is regularly provided with the opportunity to see his/her file.
Signed ....

The project also emphasizes openness here, encouraging the young person to monitor and plan his or her own performance.

Finally the parent or guardian signs – 'The terms of this contract between my son/daughter and the KEY Project have been explained to me and I agree to co-operate with the Scheme in any way that I can including receiving regular contact and visits at home.' – and is given the Project's address and telephone number, with a reminder 'In case of difficulty phone your Tracker first. If they are not available phone. . . .'

The emphasis on clarity and on writing down all agreements began at the outset when the young person and parents were given a simple question and answer leaflet. The first question on it was *What is KEY and whom is it for?*, which was answered 'KEY is a project for young people aged 14–16 who have committed offences, are due to appear in Court and are in danger of receiving a Detention Centre or Youth Custody Sentence. The KEY Project is an alternative to custody.' Then followed *What happens before my Court appearance?*, *What happens at my Court appearance?*, *What do I have to agree to do whilst on bail?* through to *But what actually happens to me whilst I'm on KEY?* and *What happens to me if I don't co-operate?* Whoever wrote the leaflet, and indeed the contracts, tried to use as lucid and direct language as possible.

In its first year of operation this intensive project worked with 16 young people, 15 boys and one girl. Ten were referred by probation and six by the social services. As well as those sent by juvenile courts in Kirklees, five were sent by the Crown Court, one on appeal. Nine had previously served custodial sentences, mostly of three months or more, and 11 had very heavy rates of previous offending. The types of offences ranged from thefts and burglaries to serious assault and arson. Of the two young people returned to court because they breached conditions, one was transferred to another of the KEY projects and the other received an absolute discharge for his breach. When he subsequently offended again, he was given a further 90 days at the project. Four of the 16 did re-offend during the duration of their supervision but only two received a custodial sentence, the other two being returned to the project. The workers identified at this stage the value of being able to continue to work with young people after the official end of their period on the scheme, to enable them to withdraw at an appropriate rather than an artificial time. However, such arrangements were always made on a voluntary basis and only on the young person's request.

The rolling programme for groups

The rationale for any unified programme for all the young people sent by the courts to schemes which are alternatives to custody is that the different elements in the programme are complementary. They will inform, teach and help all concerned. Each part of the programme can with comparative ease be structured as a separate module but the programme is followed in logical order. The subject one day, for example, can be coping with family relationships, the next day relationships with friends, or a session about the role of the police in society can be followed by a visit from a policeman. The difficulty lies in deciding how to form groups of young people to follow the course and when to slot in new entrants. A school or college curriculum is based on terms with a single point of entry and the administrators know in advance how many pupils they will have. Courts, however, usually sit weekly and it is impossible to forecast how many participants they will produce for the programmes or when.

There are obvious disadvantages, as was found at the Junction Project, in waiting to form a group until sufficient young people have been ordered to attend the scheme in any particular period, and then closing that group to others. The members of a selected group will come to know each other well, the leaders will be able to build on the relationships formed and learning may be quicker without the distraction of new entrants, but the logistics of planning the schedule are difficult. In addition, there is the problem of what to do with the young people when they first arrive. Immediate involvement is what they need and what the court usually expects, rather than a waiting period without a firm starting date.

In Kirklees the use of a 'rolling' or continuing group, joined by young people as soon as they were assigned to a project, was carefully planned. The staff were conscious from the beginning of the way the dynamics of a group would be changed by each new entrant. The newcomer in turn would need help when joining and there was also the question of how to mark each individual's exit from a group and programme that would continue afterwards. Staff for the groups rotated, with at least two workers for a maximum of six young people. To ensure continuity one member of staff always took two consecutive sessions. The week's groups were planned on Mondays and there were weekly meetings with the trackers to co-ordinate the individual schedules and to check progress. Each Friday the notes on the week's work were written up for the records, with a project leader attending for supervision. The role of visitors was scrutinized, with a minimum of one week's attendance being requested from those who wished to observe. Students were welcomed to learn about groupwork if they attended for a block of 12 weeks. The work phase of each session lasted two hours. Time spent on meals was additional.

The workers developed a module to mark entries and departures, usually lasting about an hour, within the main session. The aim was clearly stated. For young people who joined always on Mondays, it was simply to introduce them. The basic rules of the group were explained, their mutual expectations discussed and they played games to introduce all the members. The aim for those leaving, always on Thursdays, was 'to provide the young person with a positive leaving experience'. To this end the impending departure was announced at the previous session, the young person chose the games or exercises that formed part of the final session, and was given a book which everyone signed, a Mars bar and 'a tin of mushy peas to remember the snacks'. Everyone found the repetitive nature of these rituals comforting and releasing.

The actual programme was of paired sessions for each week. As has been explained, it did not matter at what point in the cycle a young person entered but the order of the sessions was fixed. The aims, content and methodology were clearly set out for the workers. Here is the resumé of one the paired sessions:

1. *Title of session*: Cartooning.
Aims: To identify decision points on a prepared cartoon and to identify alternative decisions and behaviour.

Content: Presentation of prepared cartoon of offence. Identification of decision points. Preparation of prepared cartoon of victim. Role-plays of both situations. Discussion of outcomes and/or possible outcomes. Role-play of alternative decisions and outcomes.
Method: Use cartoons; discussion; role-play; video.

2. *Title of session*: Consequences – victims.
Aims: To identify actual and possible effects upon victims of crime and to increase awareness of implication of actions.
Content: Refer to work of previous session. To examine newspaper reports of crime (real effects on victims). Examination of moral issues – 'Would they like it themselves?'. Examine costs to victim – physical, mental, economic.
Method: Challenging perceptions; role-play; video; discussion; newspaper cuttings; brainstorm [calling out suggestions and ideas one after the other].

Another linked pair of sessions were called 'Self-image' and 'Communication'. Here, in addition to discussion, role-play and use of video, they used worksheets and computer cards to encourage the young people to share their experiences and to disclose their perceptions. The aim of the session on self-image was 'to focus on young people's awareness of themselves and the effect that their image can have on other people' and the content aimed at increasing social skills to secure more positive relationships. The aim and content were reflected in the paired session on communication. By showing and practising different kinds of verbal and non-verbal communication, they learnt how responses and attitudes can be misunderstood in different situations.

Similarly, a general discussion about basic human rights and responsibilities was paired with an informative session on welfare rights, employment and unemployment, with individuals identifying their ideal job and then discussing how to go about finding it. The practical sessions, like 'survival skills in society' linked with how to identify and achieve one's own short and long-term targets, were balanced by more conceptual ones. Here is the module for the session on 'authority' paired with one centred on a visit by a magistrate.

1. *Title of session*: Authority.
Aim of session: To increase young person's awareness of the role of authority is all aspects of their life.
Content: To identify who and what authority figures are. To examine

a) the number of authority figures in each young person's life
b) how did they become involved?
c) how do you 'get rid' of them?
d) how they have affected your life.

To balance the positive and negative aspects of Authority figures i.e. *to identify the good points.*

Preparation of question cards for magistrate's visit.

Method: Brainstorm; work sheets; shadow drawing; self-disclosure; discussion; shared experience and ideas.

2. *Title of session*: Magistrate's visit.

Aim of session: An opportunity to test further pre-conceived perceptions of magistrates with someone who is in that role. To give young people a positive experience of contact with a magistrate. To provide an opportunity for dialogue.

Content: Information/talk by magistrate. Young people asking prepared questions and receiving answers. Discussion/feedback/evaluation of session.

Method: Visit by magistrate; discussion; question cards.

In the session on the family, possible areas of conflict and co-operation were explored. In that on friends, they looked at 'the positives and negatives of existing friendships' and 'what makes a good friend'. This session introduced the idea of peer-group pressure and strategies for coping with pressure to break the laws. The range of the 12 pairs of sessions was as follows, in sequence but with the starting order variable:

Cartooning: Consequences – Victim.
Self-image: Communication.
General sanctions: Legal sanctions.
Police: Police visit.
Rules, rights and responsibilities: Welfare rights, employment and
    unemployment.
Survival skills: Targets.
Authority: Magistrate's visit.
Cartooning: Consequences – Offender.
Communication: Self-image.
Detention Centre Visit (talk by former inmate or prison officer):
    Survival skills.
Family: Friends.
Police and Criminal Evidence Bill – information about the legislation
    brought into force in 1987 – 'On the Streets': PACE 'In the Station'.

The programme for the groups thus focused on offending behaviour but also tackled their general development as young people coping with the pressures of growing up, the two aspects being linked. The topics in themselves were appropriate for an ordinary social studies course in any secondary school, but the angle from which they were approached was different.

The National Children's Centre Project

The young people who attended the National Children's Centre project at Milnsbridge, Huddersfield, where the National Children's Centre was already based, would probably otherwise have been sent into custody for a short spell or been given a Care Order for offending. In addition, they also had severe problems about attending school either because they were persistent truants or because they had been suspended from their schools. The project tried to tackle both the offending and the school problem. The document explaining the venture puts the emphasis thus: 'The day care provision at the National Children's Centre aims primarily to introduce a structured framework to the young person's day, at the same time as initiating a change in their specific offending behaviour.'

To achieve its dual aim the project used groupwork, education and work experience for older participants who were approaching school-leaving age: mainly painting and decorating, joinery and gardening, at the project and in the community. The content of the groupwork programme included 'offending, school, family and leisure. Much of the time is spent concentrating on the offending behaviour of the young people, and challenging their attitudes and beliefs with regard to their offences.'

The educational programme had three elements. First there was the acquisition of basic educational skills, according to individual needs. The project in the short time available offered some remedial education, helping the young person to catch up on some of the work that had been missed. One of the factors which often inhibits truants and reluctant pupils from returning to class is that they know they will feel lost, embarrassed and 'stupid' because they have missed so much. The longer they are away from school, the worse this feeling grows. Filling the gaps in their knowledge was thus not only useful in itself but also might help their return to school.

Secondly, the project offered work linked with what they would have been doing at that time in their class at school, liaising with their teachers. Thirdly, and most important, the project tried to re-integrate the young person gradually into school, after careful negotiations with the school and according to individual needs and progress. The project leader, Moira Swann, had a background in both teaching and social work. She worked with two full-time and one part-time members of staff and a part-time clerical and administrative officer.

Young people and their parents signed a brief contract which again made clear that if they failed 'to uphold the demands of the project' they might be returned to court, and in all cases a report was sent to the court when the young person completed the order. Again there was a simple leaflet, this time with amusing line drawings, asking and answering questions like *Are there any holidays?* (Answer: '*In school holidays members attend the project for two days a week.*') Rules given include:

SMOKING is allowed in canteen area if parents approve.

CLEANING – all members help maintain the premises.

MEALS are provided at the project, but must be paid for by the young person, 35p for main meal, snacks are available.

'Group targets' are given as:

1 No offending whilst at KEY.
2 Help others to achieve No. 1.

The leaflet also gave the bus routes from Huddersfield bus station since, like the other two KEY projects, this one served all Kirklees. Public transport in Kirklees was good, with buses serving all the centres, so workers rarely had to fetch or return young people to their homes. They saw it as part of the programme for young people that they should take responsibility for getting themselves on time to the project or wherever they were meant to be. No young person's journey took more than an hour and they were given their fares.

Most of those who attended the project had numerous or serious offences and attended school for less than a third of the time they should. In the first year there were 13 boys and two girls. Twelve were offenders and three did not attend school at all. Only one was referred by the educational social work service, six by social services and eight by probation. The majority had between ten and 40 offences or were appearing for a serious offence like robbery. Only one boy from the first year's intake ended in custody after re-offending. Another received a second community-based alternative to custody at the Children's Society

KEY project. The three young people returned to court for breaching the conditions of their orders went back to the project.

The project worked with young people from nine different schools in its first year. Six young people were not attending school at all at the time of their court appearance, two were suspended from school and two were changing from special to mainstream education. During the first year it became clear that non-offenders should not be included at the project just because of their problems in attending school. It was also decided to increase links with the community and to reduce the amount of time spent at the centre. Although schools were generally co-operative and supportive towards the young people at KEY, liaison and re-integration of the young people into schools was far from easy. The schools had regard to the majority of their pupils as well as the needs of the minority of difficult and disruptive pupils.

It can be seen that in many ways the problems the KEY project met were similar to those faced by all off-site education projects which aim to return young people to school, but the KEY project had the added difficulty that all its young people were offenders. The question to be answered for the future was whether it was effective to tackle together the two problems of offending and non-attendance at school, even if the two were linked.

Barnardo's Alternatives to Custody and Care Project

The third KEY project set up through the DHSS 1983 initiative in Kirklees was designed for persistent young offenders likely to receive a short Detention Centre Order or a Care Order. It was a Barnardo's project, originally based at Dryfield House in Batley, a former children's home, and then at Northorpe Hall, Mirfield, in an attractive, rural setting. Northorpe Hall had been used extensively since the early 1970s as a centre for family casework and residential weekends for young people, and the Northorpe Hall Trust had been one of the early pioneers of Intermediate Treatment.

In the description of the project, Tony Homer, the project leader, explained that the main aim of the programme was to change established patterns of offending. The methods used by the staff of project leader and three full-time workers, with part-time clerical and administrative support, were group work and individual counselling. The sessions for the groups, as in the other KEY projects, challenged delinquent attitudes and encouraged young people 'to employ other, more socially acceptable means of responding to the pressures that they face in everyday life'. By looking at personal problems, whether at home or in school, the individual counsellors also reinforced the work done in groups.

The young people attended two evenings a week for three months, under a Supervision Order with a specified activities clause (Section 12(3)c of the CYPA 1969). An undertaking was given to return the young person to court if he or she were in breach of the conditions, and this was explained in the 'formal agreement' signed by young person, parents, supervising officer and KEY staff. The young person's agreement – the word 'contract' was avoided at this project – began by stating 'I have committed an offence of . . . . and have agreed to attend the KEY project which will allow me to remain at home under the conditions of a one year Supervision Order with a "specified activity" clause.' The supervising officer agreed to maintain supervision during the period as well as to keep in regular contact, and the KEY commitment emphasized responsibility for communicating with everyone.

The distinctive features of this project were that it included children from the age of ten (although most were over 15) and more young people were eligible for it. In its first year it worked with 34 young people, as usual with far more boys than girls: 31 boys and only three girls. Twenty-three were referred by probation and 11 by social services. Two came from Crown Courts, the rest from juvenile courts. Some had five or six previous appearances in court and others were at risk of custody because of the nature of their offences. All seven who were in breach of their conditions of attendance at the project during the year were returned to the project by the courts to complete their programmes, which they then did. However, more than at the other projects, nine in all, re-offended and were then sent into custody, although two others were placed on the Children's Society Tracking Project.

As well as working with the young people, the project had regular contact with their families, 'keeping them informed about what is going on and giving them an opportunity to take a positive role in helping the young person stay out of trouble'. It found a parents' support group useful, although difficult to fit into the busy schedule of the staff. Mainly mothers attended and the group was open to former as well as current parents. The group met once a fortnight at the project base in Batley, in the poorer end of Kirklees, also easy to reach from Dewsbury. The parents, from six to nine in number usually, liked sharing their troubles but preferred the project workers to suggest the programme or topics for discussion, not having the confidence to do so themselves. Attendance was voluntary, not part of any prior condition for the young person's attendance, so they were a self-selected group and may not have included the parents who needed most help with their children. But in general the group was seen as worth developing.

The policy of KEY projects to accept all appropriate referrals put special pressure on this project because of the number of young people who were eligible for it, but the rolling programme for groups was again found to be a satisfactory way to take in constant new referrals. There was no residential element in this or the other KEY projects. It would have been difficult to fit weekends or periods away into the rolling programmes of the groups and the staff were in any case doubtful about the value for their young people of what they called 'the outward bound' approach.

The impact of KEY

In the report marking the end of KEY as a three-year project, KEY's success is defined: 'According to what we would regard as the most significant criteria of success (i.e. whether or not young people were able to maintain their place in the community and be dealt with appropriately in that context), the Projects have proved to be successful and viable.' The figures quoted substantiate this claim. Not only did most of those on KEY projects manage to complete their orders in the community, but fewer of them re-offended within two years than those sent into custody by local courts in the same period. The report anticipates the argument that those given custodial rather than community disposals may have been the hardened cases, more likely to re-offend, explaining that sometimes the young people who came to KEY had more serious previous offending. Although over two-thirds of those at KEY projects had committed offences against property, mainly burglary, about 15 per cent had used some kind of violence.

Evidence of the effectiveness of the projects with regard to offending was now available for magistrates, elected representatives, local authority administrators and the general public in Kirklees. During the three years, 153 young people had been through the projects, of whom only seven were girls and only three were under 14 years of age (under

Care Orders for offending), 83 being 14 or 15 and 67 aged 16 or 17. The Probation Service, which dealt with court matters for those of 13 and over, had referred almost two-thirds, and social services the others (mainly young people they already knew or were supervising), except for two referred by the education social work service. Only 18 did not complete their time on a KEY project, so by the criterion of attendance the success rate was 88 per cent. In all 26 young people were returned to court for breaching conditions of their orders and all but one subsequently completed their time at KEY. The comparisons on re-offending between those sent to KEY and those sent to custody were:

Re-offended within two years After KEY 62%

            After custody 81%

Sent into custody within two years After KEY 19%

            After custody 43%

The reduction in the number of young people given custodial disposals over the period was marked. We have seen that in 1983 Kirklees courts were sending into custody 21 per cent of male 14–16 year-olds before them, compared with a national average of 12 per cent. By 1985 the percentage had dropped to 13 per cent, only 2 per cent above the national average for that year, and the number of young people from 118 to 59. In 1986 only 26 Custodial Orders were made. These figures have to be viewed in the context of the drop in the number of young people appearing in the courts, through demographic changes in the number of young people in the population and through the introduction of cautioning panels over the whole area by January 1986. However, the corresponding increase in the proportion of Supervision Orders made, from only 7 per cent in 1983 to 16 per cent, near the national average of 17 per cent, in 1985 shows that there had been a shift in the sentencing pattern. It was also reflected in an increase in the number of Community Service Orders made: 18 in 1985 compared with none in 1983. Most important, the courts had accepted 69 per cent of recommendations to KEY projects made in social inquiry reports.

The final report analysed the factors which had assisted the achievements of the three KEY projects and led to their integration into the permanent provision for young people by Kirklees. On the structural side, it noted first the initial commitment of the local authority Social Services Committee to the enterprise. The complex management system, with the project workers employed by the three voluntary agencies but with the local authority manager, Mark Feeny, responsible for the practice of the projects, had given a breadth of approach and experience. The independence of KEY outside the statutory system had left it free to be innovative and the involvement of all the agencies in the area had facilitated overall planning.

As for practice, clarity of aims was crucial. The projects had identified and kept to their target group. From the outset they had allowed time to be spent on publicizing their services, to the social workers and probation officers who might refer young people (including an annual study day), and to the magistrates who had to know the details and strengths of the alternatives to custody and care that were offered. They had also monitored and refined their practice as they went, spending time on staff training. The Save the Children Fund Hilltop Project, conveniently near, had been involved throughout in a consultancy role, and had given training to the individual teams for their different approaches.

There had also been difficulties, some of them the reverse side of the advantages. For instance, the independence of the voluntary organiz-ations running the projects slowed the process of agreeing changes, as these had to be explained through all the hierarchies and brought into line with their general policies. The overall lack of good enough facilities for young people often put pressure on the projects to accept young people who were not necessarily on the brink of custody but who needed supervision, with activities in the community which were not available elsewhere. Nor had KEY been put forward as an alternative for all those at risk of custody. Between July 1984 and December 1986 there were 56 probation cases and 21 social services cases not referred to KEY, nearly a quarter in fact of all cases of young people at risk of a custodial disposal. The project workers logically argued that if the magistrates did not see a reference to KEY in a report, they would assume that the young person was thought unsuitable for community referral, rather than that the option had not been considered.

One problem the workers were aware of but had been unable to tackle was their lack of experience to meet the needs of the small number of black young people who attended the projects. The 1981 census showed that 8 per cent of the population of Kirklees lived in households with the head born in the New Commonwealth or Pakistan. In the north of the area the figure was 23 per cent and, as in general among communities from the ethnic minorities, the proportion of young people was higher than in the total population. The northern area was also the most deprived area, with the highest percentage of children in single parent households. More West Indian people lived in Huddersfield, more from the Asian communities in Dewsbury and Batley. Only six young people from ethnic minorities had attended KEY projects, but because there was no monitoring of ethnic origin it was not known how many had passed through the courts or into custody. The projects had no black workers and the staff were aware that they had less knowledge, confidence and rapport in dealing with the few young people who attended from ethnic minorities and their families. Without a statistical base to know how many black young people were involved in the juvenile justice system no action seemed possible.

A strategy for juvenile justice

The KEY projects were introduced as part of a developing strategy in Kirklees. The DHSS 1983 initiative gave the various agencies a timely fillip and welcome financial aid, but the projects were rooted in the local authority's long-term plans for children and young people. Nor did they exist in isolation. They were the alternatives to custody and care which complemented a Family Support Centre (to help prevent the breaking up of families), Kirklees Project for Girls, the Northorpe Barn Project and the work of the Adoption and Fostering Unit. Kirklees Project for Girls offered an integrated service for difficult girls, including an Assessment Unit, Mentor families (specially trained foster parents who received a salary in addition to the boarding-out allowance) and an Independent Living Unit. Some of the services had been developed in partnership with voluntary agencies and they had been introduced at different times, with funding from a variety of sources.

In the paper put before the Social Services Committee in July 1986, the totality of the strategy, seeking community care instead of residential care as a general principle, was demonstrated by quoting the figures for children in care as well as those for the numbers in custody:

	In care	In community homes	In CHEs
1981	1041	251	74
1986	548	72	21

The aim now was to provide an integrated service for children and young people in Kirklees. The KEY Projects were to be subsumed into this, taken over completely by the local authority, with the former Children's Society Tracking Project and the Barnardo's Project retaining their different approaches for those at risk of long and short periods of custody, and the former National Children's Centre Project broadening into a general project for re-integrating children into school.

Thus the three former KEY projects officially became part of a chain of resources. The starting point was diversion as advocated in the 1980 white paper *Young Offenders*: 'All the available evidence suggests that juvenile offenders who can be diverted from the criminal justice system at an early stage in their offending are less likely to re-offend than those who become involved in judicial proceedings.' The first project, based at Northorpe Barn, would be for young people aged from 10 to 17 who had begun offending, had perhaps been cautioned by the police, and who might be prosecuted again unless they received some outside help. The aim was to work with them for as short a period as possible, no longer than six weeks, but in that time to examine the young person's behaviour with him or her and the family. They might be helped to make an apology or some form of reparation to a victim and they would be referred where possible to youth groups and other informal agencies.

The next resource was to be for those given Supervision Orders without provision for Intermediate Treatment. One full-time member of staff with a budget for sessional helpers would offer from Northorpe Barn an advisory and consultancy service to supervising officers throughout Kirklees. The aim would be to work across agency boundaries and to collate information about all the facilities available for young people in Kirklees. The officer would also be able to consider new methods of implementing Supervision Orders, like using people in the community to befriend young offenders. There was a dual purpose here in making sure that young people were introduced to facilities in the community and in encouraging the development of new resources.

The project to re-integrate young people into school was to be based on the former KEY National Children's Centre project and indeed to have the same leader, but it was to be extended to non-offenders at risk of being sent away to CHEs (Community Homes with Education) because they did not attend school, and to those returning home from CHEs. Fourteen young people at any one time would work a maximum of two days a week from 9.30 a.m. to 4.00 p.m. at the Reintegration to School Resource, and a minimum of three days a week in school, for up to two terms. The main difference from the KEY project was that the work would focus entirely on returning to school and not address offending as such nor be offered as an alternative to Custody or Care Orders. Those who were offenders would attend one of the other projects in the evenings for that aspect of their lives. Although it was to be a social services resource, the partnership with the education service was emphasized by the financial contribution of the education service, initially £29,000 a year.

A major part of the task would lie in building good relations with teachers in the eight schools in Kirklees from which most of the young people came, and with the teachers in Kirklees' existing disruption unit, attended by difficult pupils still on school rolls. There is a tradition of strictness in West Yorkshire schools which mirrors the toughness of family discipline. The cane was often used until banned. Many families resort to good hidings, saying to the social workers 'I keep telling them at the school they should hit him. Then he'd behave all right'. The Reintegration to School Resource took a different approach when it began in its new form in October 1987, encouraging the young people to 'make a friend of your teacher' and vice versa. Another of its roles was in helping the educational welfare service develop new ways to cope with children when they began truanting, including special groups for them. For those young people for whom a return to school was not feasible, the Resource would offer a vocational programme including tuition in literacy, numeracy, communication skills and looking for jobs as well as work experience. All the staff were women, except for a part-time craft teacher, and they had found no problems about discipline, even with the toughest, 'macho' boys.

The first of the resources intended specifically for the courts to use was for young people aged from ten to 17 who had already been given a Supervision Order but who, through further offending, needed more stringent supervision under a 12-month Supervision Order with an Intermediate Treatment clause (Section 12(2) CYPA 1969). A maximum of 20 young people at any one time would attend a small group for one or two evenings a week for six months. The groups would focus on examining offending behaviour and developing social skills.

Next, the courts would have two alternatives to custody and care, based substantially on the two KEY projects run by the Children's Society and Barnardo's. As before, the first would be an alternative to short custodial sentences of under four months and the second to longer ones. The numbers envisaged were up to 20 young people at any one time, boys aged 14 to 17 and girls aged 15 to 17. The less intensive alternative would operate under a one year Supervision Order with a Specified Activities clause, last three months and use groupwork two evenings a week at the centre and individual sessions twice a week away from the centre. The more intensive alternative would again use a period of 28 days on conditional bail to secure co-operation, followed by a one year Supervision Order with a Specified Activities clause. The course would last four months, using tracking as previously and intensive groupwork two evenings a week.

For the parents of young people on the projects offering alternatives to custody and care, there would be a support group as run previously and it was planned to develop work as necessary, in agreement with the young person's supervising officer, to wean individual young people gradually from the project after their statutory attendance was over. One member of staff would be assigned to draw up individual programmes for young people still likely to be given Care Orders for offending. Very much against the national trend, 20 of these orders had been made in 1985 and five Charge and Control Restrictions had been imposed on existing Care Orders. Charge and Control Restrictions, generally known as Residential Care Orders, were introduced in 1983 for young people who had previously been given Care Orders for offending and who had offended again. The restriction was on their being placed at home. Contrary to expectation, the disposal has not been used frequently. Only 21 orders were made during 1986 in England and Wales.

A new facility to be offered the courts was a Community Remand Resource. The aim would be to reduce the number of young people remanded in residential care or in custody whilst waiting to appear before Kirklees juvenile or Crown courts, whether for trial of contested cases or disposal of their case after reports. The only juveniles who can be remanded in custody are boys of 15 and over who have been certified as unruly by the court, on strict condition that no other course is possible for the protection of the public. In 1984 the Yorkshire and Humberside region made 27 per cent of all the certificates of unruly character issued nationally, although the base population of the region constituted only 10.5 per cent of the national population. During 1985, 61 young people were remanded in custody and 60 in care. It was planned to offer realistic alternatives to residential or custodial placements by providing a high level of supervision and support for young people, to minimize the risk of further offending whilst on remand and to ensure attendance at court when required.

Two full-time and two part-time workers would be able to work with about 15 young people at any one time, contacting them every day. The young people would have been remanded into the care of the local authority or initially remanded in custody, but subsequently released by the court into care for the Community Remand. The return home would be viewed as a positive means to reduce re-offending for the future, not just as a temporary expedient. During the time on remand the worker would begin to examine with the young person and family past behaviour and future options, as well as to liaise with all those involved, from solicitors to schools.

Finally, it was planned to monitor by computer this range of complementary resources to ensure that all were being used as intended and to identify new trends. The effect of social inquiry reports would be charted. Those working on the juvenile justice projects would continue to be involved in general training within the social services department and in liaison work with other agencies.

The re-organization changed the basis of employment for the three leaders of the KEY projects and the five full-time and seven part-time workers. Under the new arrangements the Manager of the three KEY projects, Mark Feeny, who was already working for Kirklees Social Services Department, became Principal Officer, Juvenile Justice, responsible through the Development Manager for Children and Families to the Assistant Director for Fieldwork and Domiciliary Services. The three former KEY project leaders each now became Principal Social Workers, Juvenile Justice, heading three sections. Barbara Martin, formerly of the Children's Society, was in charge of the Remand Project, the Cautioning Project and the Supervision Support Project; Tony Homer, formerly of Barnardo's, was in charge of the Alternative to Custody and Care Projects; and Moira Swann, formerly of the National Children's Centre, was in charge of the Education Project and the Supervision with Intermediate Treatment Project. In addition there were two court officers.

Such a re-organization, successful in the case of Kirklees, raises general issues about the conditions of employment of many working with young offenders who may come from different professions and different sectors, with their own salary scales and entitlements. Some may be former social workers or teachers, others former youth and community workers. Some may not have formal qualifications but may have entered the field through residential social work or volunteering. The big voluntary organizations like the Children's Society and Barnardo's have composite grades for their social workers, and the individual worker negotiates his or her point of entry into the scale on joining the organization. These grades may not always be compatible with those in local authority social services departments. Time-limited projects, like the three KEY projects and others set up under the DHSS LAC(83)

117

initiative, offer their staff limited contracts. Not all pension rights were portable from one profession to another up till recently, and staff may lose seniority on changing to the scale of another profession. There is no specific qualification for working with young offenders and those at risk and, perhaps as a consequence, there are no nationally agreed scales of remuneration. As a result it is often hard for those involved to plan satisfactory careers.

Key features

Although some of the features of provision for juvenile offenders in Kirklees changed with the integration of the three KEY projects into the Social Services Department, the services developed logically over time. The new strategy was founded on multi-agency co-operation and general planning for children and families, which began before the 1983 DHSS initiative gave the opportunity to extend the alternatives to custody and care. Kirklees had special reason to take advantage of that initiative because of the high rates for custody and care in the area. The main features in Kirklees can be summarized as follows.

- An integrated strategy for young offenders throughout Kirklees, part of the area's planning for all young people.
- Emphasis on preventive work to divert young people from the courts and care.
- Careful 'gate-keeping' and separation of different kinds of offenders.
- Specific project for those not attending school, at first as an alternative to custody for those also offending but subsequently an educational resource under social services management.
- Graduated projects for different types of supervision orders. Two projects as alternatives to custody and care, the more intensive including trackers whose role is to act as counsellor as well as to contain the young person and prevent re-offending.
- Contracts for all concerned with a clear statement of action to be taken if conditions are breached.
- Continuous or 'rolling' group programmes used to tackle offending behaviour and to increase social and life skills.
- No residential courses or active sports.
- No specialists attached to the projects but use of community facilities like child guidance.
- Regular internal training.

- Probation involved from the age of 13.
- Monitoring of the system, with supervision of reports to the courts made by social services, but a less formal arrangement for reports made by the probation service.
- Emphasis on publicity within social services, education and other agencies and for the juvenile and Crown courts.
- Regular reporting back to the courts.

5

Tracking

The West Sussex Scheme

The West Sussex Tracking Scheme was set up under the DHSS 1983 initiative which provided short-term finance for the creation of new alternatives to custody and care by voluntary agencies in co-operation with local authorities. Of 110 schemes approved under the initiative, it was one of only four which by December 1987 had been discontinued and not integrated into the local authority's permanent provision for Intermediate Treatment. In order to see why it was discontinued, and thus failed to meet one of the primary aims of the initiative, it is necessary to look first at how it was established and why.

In 1982 the Social Services Committee in West Sussex made an agreement with the Probation Committee for the area about how to implement the new Criminal Justice Act 1982 and in particular about providing schemes of Intermediate Treatment for those given Supervision Orders with specified activities under what had become Section 12(3)c of the Children and Young Persons Act 1969. West Sussex was divided into three areas. The North Eastern Division included the towns of Crawley, Horsham, East Grinstead and Haywards Heath. The Southern Division covered Littlehampton, Worthing and the area up to the south-eastern border with East Sussex. The Western Division contained Bognor Regis, Chichester, Midhurst, Petworth and the surrounding rural areas. The highest concentration of population, and of juvenile crime, was in the North Eastern Division, the lowest in the Western Division.

The arrangement was that Probation should be responsible in the North Eastern Division for all Supervision Orders with supervised activities and for other Supervision Orders made for criminal offences for young people aged over 13. Probation in the Southern Division again took all Supervision Orders with supervised activities but the Social

Services Department was responsible for other Supervision Orders. In the Western Division, social services were responsible for all provision, including any alternatives to custody or care under Supervision Orders with specified activities. As it was a statutory responsibility of a social services department to provide facilities for Intermediate Treatment, social services in West Sussex gave Probation the budget they would have spent on Intermediate Treatment posts and support, about £48,000 a year. The advantage of this arrangement was that the Home Office matched with additional money any funds local Probation committees acquired in their own areas. Through this arrangement Probation in West Sussex therefore increased the amount of revenue it had available for all its work.

The arrival of the DHSS circular LAC(83)3 in January 1983 gave an opportunity for the Social Services Department to develop its alternatives to custody, but responsibility for these had already been given in two areas to probation. Bognor Regis, Chichester, Midhurst and Petworth, the towns in the remaining area, are not generally associated with heavy crime. At the end of the Tracking Scheme the Social Services Committee was told that the workload for Supervision Orders with supervised activities at any one time, was nine young offenders in the North Eastern Division, eight in Southern and only six in Western, and the figures for Supervision Orders in general were 87, 70 and 57 respectively. Nevertheless, a case was made in order to launch the venture for providing alternative facilities in the community for those at risk of custody and care who lived in the Western Division.

Why was a tracking scheme chosen? Whatever form of scheme was adopted, in order to qualify for the DHSS initiative it had to be intensive, and for those at risk of custody or care. The adoption of tracking rather than a more conventional approach was suggested by the Divisional Director in the Western area. Apart from his enthusiasm for the method of work, the introductory leaflet about the scheme for social workers, magistrates and others explained that a tracking scheme had been chosen because it enabled the whole of the available grant to be invested in personnel as opposed to premises and equipment. 'Also, since the area to be covered by the scheme takes in three petty-sessional divisions (Chichester, Midhurst and Petworth), a tracking approach offered greater flexibility, and therefore far more frequent and intensive contact with each Young Offender than a scheme operating in one central location.'

Eventually Chichester Diocesan Association for Family Social Work was the voluntary agency which agreed to manage the scheme, sponsored by West Sussex Social Services Department according to the conditions of the DHSS initiative. The involvement of a Church of England diocesan organization was interesting. Although diocesan organizations generally had many interests in preventive schemes for children and young people at risk, only two others sponsored alternative to custody schemes under the DHSS initiative. The main reason for the Chichester Diocesan Association's involvement was that its Children's Centre at Knowles Tooth near Hurstpierpoint ran residential courses and group meetings for young people on Intermediate Treatment schemes in East and West Sussex. The work undertaken at Knowles Tooth was described in *A Measure of Diversion?* by Robert Adam, Simon Allard, John Baldwin and Jim Thomas, published by the National Youth Bureau in 1981. The Association's Director, Neil Morgan, who was also a local magistrate, had worked earlier in his career at Northorpe Hall in Kirklees and thus had long experience as well as interest in Intermediate Treatment.

The framework

A full-time team consisting of Project Leader and four trackers accepted referrals, from 1 January 1985, of 14 to 16 year olds in the Western Division 'convicted and sentenced by the Juvenile Court as a direct alternative to a custodial sentence'. Social workers and probation officers when preparing social inquiry reports were invited to refer offenders to the Project Leader for consideration. If the referral was accepted, and the Supervision Order with a requirement for specified activities made by the court, the supervisor remained responsible for the continuing supervision of the offender under the court order and for liaison with the project team. If magistrates wanted to consider the scheme for an individual and the scheme had not been recommended in the report on the young person, they were asked to adjourn the case for two weeks to enable the offender to be assessed.

The tracking element in the scheme was more intensive than that undertaken in the KEY projects of Kirklees. Some of its features were modelled on the Leeds alternative to custody scheme which staff visited. For a period of three months the young offenders would report to their trackers up to three times a day, seven days a week. In addition, they would attend group sessions twice a week in Bognor, where the project was based, or in Chichester, and would attend residential courses of at least three days every month. 'The emphasis, especially at first', the introductory leaflet explained, 'is on discipline and conformity. Once a routine is established, the Tracker will use some of the reporting-interviews to work with the offender on any specific problem area (e.g. unemployment, illiteracy, addiction, behavioural problems etc.).' Offenders who failed to conform to the Scheme's requirements would be brought back before the court. At the end of the three months, the project team, supervising officer and young offender would decide what follow-up work was necessary by the supervisor for the remainder of the Supervision Order and whether other forms of Intermediate Treatment were necessary.

Potential users of the Scheme were told that tracking was likely to be effective for several reasons: its intensity in reinforcing rules and inculcating a structured life-style; its authority through the courts with sanctions available for breaking conditions; and its positive role in maintaining and improving relationships with family, school or work. By contrast, custodial sentences were costly, had high rates of re-offending, disrupted education or work and tended to increase criminal knowledge and attitudes.

The groups were originally planned to be of between six and ten young people who would complete the programme together. This method of organization would have meant some waiting a short time for their programme to begin, but they would have been closely supervised in the interval. It was hoped to have three programmes a year, enabling the Scheme to take 30 young people a year. In fact, because of the small number of young people eligible for the Scheme (only 15 attended in the first year), a single, rolling programme was operated, with young people joining as soon as the disposal was made by the court. Residential programmes were implemented when there were sufficient young people ready. The Scheme was not completely open to all at risk of custody or care as it would not accept those considered to be a danger to themselves or to others, those without a satisfactory place to live or those with psychological or emotional problems 'which are beyond the scope of the Scheme', but during the period no young person facing custody went to court without the offer of a tracking programme.

An interesting difference between the West Sussex Tracking Scheme and the other projects considered so far in this book is that none of the staff was a qualified social worker. They came instead from a background of youth and community work or residential work with children. John Platten, the Project Leader, had a diploma in youth and community work and had previously been a community development officer and youth worker. Two team members had worked extensively in residential care, a third had entered Intermediate Treatment as a volunteer and another youth worker had become involved in Intermediate Treatment on a sessional basis. Part of their success with families, they thought, stemmed from the fact that they were not seen as adjuncts of social services but as people committed solely to helping the young people. There had not, however, originally been a positive plan to recruit a team from outside the social services. What happened was that the advertisements for the posts had not specified any particular qualifications and the salaries offered were too low, except for the post of Project Leader, to attract any but newly-qualified social workers. The only people with the right experience who applied were not social workers. This feature of the team thus evolved almost by accident.

The Scheme demanded much involvement from families. The leaflet to parents of young people being considered for the Scheme explained that parents would be asked first, with the young person, to meet the project staff and a social worker or probation officer to assess the young person's suitability for the Scheme. They would then be asked to sign a form giving the conditions of the Scheme, confirming their support of their child on the Scheme and 'thus enabling the young person to meet the conditions of the Scheme'. They were asked to participate in the monthly reviews of their child's progress and to liaise with the tracker regularly. It was also made clear what would happen if conditions were breached. As the Scheme evolved, groups for parents were established. The meetings were planned to enable the parents to give each other mutual support as well as for the staff to give information and report progress.

The conditions signed by the young person began 'I understand that the Tracking Scheme is an alternative to the Court sending me into custody or into care.' In addition to agreeing to maintain contact with the tracker as instructed and to attend all sessions as required, the young person agreed 'to conduct myself in a responsible way and to be of good behaviour whilst on the Scheme. I understand that aggressive behaviour towards other clients or staff will not be tolerated, and that it is unacceptable to be under the influence of drugs, drink or solvents.' The consequences of breaching the conditions were also spelt out and the project staff in turn signed an undertaking to provide a programme 'with the object of enabling . . . to work towards more constructive alternatives to his/her offending behaviour'.

Tracking in action

John Platten's report of August 1986, after the Scheme had been in existence for 18 months and was already shadowed by uncertainty about its future, contains lively portraits of the Scheme in action. In its second year of operation the workers introduced training in sailing as an activity. The T. S. Larvik was a forty-foot gaff rigger, which had formerly been in the Norwegian Coastguard Service, and had then been taken over by the Manpower Services Commission and East Sussex County Council. Moored in Brighton Marina, it offered young people an introduction to sailing on short three-day trips along the south coast. Before going to sea the crew gave a full day's training in practical seamanship and safety.

The trips were used for some of the residential programmes in order to encourage teamwork and better relationships with others. 'On a forty-foot boat in the middle of the Channel there are not many places to hide, if, as often happens, things go wrong. Living in close proximity to 12 others for three days can cause an added strain. Coping with yourself and others in such a situation is a skill; learning to cope is an important experience.'

Platten took as an example Charlie Smith, sent to the Scheme after a spate of offences of criminal damage. Charlie's tracker thought, after working with Charlie and his family, that although Charlie's relationship with his father was important to him it was not satisfactory. His Dad put up barriers between himself and Charlie, blocking Charlie out and using his involvement with his Mum and the younger children to justify his attitude. Charlie was not too keen on the idea of the boat trip but his Dad liked it and when invited to accompany Charlie jumped at the chance. As soon as Charlie realized his Dad wanted to go he became keen, too.

The tracker had the specific brief to observe the interaction between father and son on the trip and how they communicated, both verbally and non-verbally. He could then try to interpret what he had learnt in the light of the information he already had about the family and use it for future work with them. In this case the trip gave father and son the opportunity to tackle tasks together and the sea was a great leveller. They saw each other in a new light and with new respect. Platten comments that it might seem unusual to have taken the father along but by doing so they found the key for that particular boy and his family.

Another feature of the scheme in its second year was reporting back to the juvenile bench half-way through and at the end of each young person's tracking programme. The reports were displayed in the magistrates' retiring rooms at the courts, enabling those magistrates who had made the orders to see how they were progressing and other magistrates to learn about the Scheme. The reports covered the general attitude of the young person on the Scheme, the frequency of contact with the tracker, the work undertaken in groups and on residential courses, and they evaluated the progress made.

In some areas magistrates consider it not appropriate for them to follow the progress of the young people they see in court or monitor the effect of disposals in individual cases. They see their role as limited to making decisions on the bench. Parliament has given the local authority or the Probation Service the responsibility of carrying out the orders made by the court and it is argued that for magistrates to be involved further is an infringement of social work independence and a confusion of the judicial function. The magistrates in West Sussex, however, found it a helpful practice and without doubt it contributed to their increasing use of the scheme and their support of it when it was threatened with closure. The practice of reporting back is spreading and in most areas those concerned confirm that they can keep a correct balance between communication and surveillance, and can maintain confidentiality.

The scheme also developed its work with families in greater depth. The project workers often found, as in the case of Charlie Smith, that the attitude of the parents towards their son or daughter was a determining factor in whether the young person could change his or her pattern of behaviour. They identified different situations in which they could intervene. Sometimes offences had been directed against members of the family and conciliation was necessary. At other times the difficulty was that parents saw the young person as out of their control and therefore wanted to abrogate their responsibility. They could be helped to take appropriate control and thus reception into care could be avoided. Another scenario was when offending seemed related to the family's dissatisfaction with the child or to the child's reaction to family problems. Parents could be helped to make positive as well as negative comments, a mother could be asked to address her son directly instead of always referring to him in the third person and never talking to him. Usually the tracker co-ordinated with the project leader to work together with the family as a whole.

The logistics of the actual tracking were that the tracker met the young person at least once a day and usually also spoke on the telephone once or twice a day in the early stages of the programme. This routine was for 362 days a year, every day except Christmas Day, Boxing Day and New

Year's Day. The trackers sometimes had to travel long distances, by car or moped, as well as working long hours. One boy lived as far away as Selsey. Each tracking programme was different, planned for each individual and reviewed every 30 days to break the period of the 90 day order into three phases, 'induction', 'middle' and 'ending'.

The group meetings were held on two evenings a week. For a short period there was an additional session on Sunday afternoons. The meetings lasted two hours and counted as one of the daily contacts on the day concerned. The discussions covered individual offences, the reasons why offences had been committed, the effects of offending on other people, how the offences could have been avoided, attitudes to the law and the future of each participant. A life and social skills programme included budgeting, health issues, racism, sexism, help with literacy, numeracy and the job market. The young people looked at videos on relevant topics, did exercises and played educational games and sometimes were involved in outside activities like sponsored walks for charity. They joined the library and went regularly with staff to take out books. There were gardening, car and computer projects. The maximum number of young people in a group was eight. The changing composition of the groups created some difficulties, as it did on some other projects which used the same system.

All the staff undertook a basic course in literacy and numeracy to equip them to work on these skills with the young people. Unemployment was a major issue but some jobs were available in the Bognor area. One young man who had failed to find employment after several unsuccessful interviews was taken on as an office junior for the Scheme, through a local Youth Training Scheme. With this experience he obtained a permanent job in local industry.

In its second year the project began to invite guests from the community to talk to the groups. They included a bank employee to explain legal ways of financing hobbies and money matters generally. The speaker who made the most impact, however, was an ex-offender who described how he began as a juvenile offender and ended, after numerous convictions and prison sentences, serving six years for manslaughter. Sometimes the effect of outside speakers recounting their experiences in jail provokes a response of bravado in a group – this was found at the Junction Project on occasion, as Maureen Stone recorded in her study – but this visitor moved his audience and enabled them to see the consquences on his life of his actions.

The residential courses included, as well as the sailing scheme, opportunities to learn sports (like bowling, ice-skating, canoeing and raft-making) and skills (like basic mechanics and using a video camera). There were no problems about attendance or participation in the activities and no serious difficulties with behaviour on the courses. The workers attributed their success here to close supervision, with two to three members of staff on each course; close relationships between staff and young people; a pre-planned, tightly structured programme (of everything, from the catering to the activities); participation by the young people in the planning and shared responsibility for the tasks; and the positive feeling engendered because all the activities were seen as constructive. The young people had more opportunities on the courses to show their strengths than they had ever been given previously and began to view people in authority in a less negative way. Some had never been out of their home town so a visit to a bigger place like Brighton could be a chastening experience, making them want to walk close to the workers for reassurance rather than assert themselves. In addition to the Knowles Tooth Centre, the scheme used Cobnor Activities Centre in Chichester Harbour.

An additional feature of the West Sussex Tracking Scheme was its contribution to the establishment of a Bail Condition Support Scheme. This enabled young offenders accused of serious crimes, or with the kind of record of previous offences or of absconding that might preclude bail, to live at home while waiting for their court appearances instead of being placed in residential care. The condition of their bail was that they reported to the Tracking Scheme up to three times a day whilst on the period of remand. They might also have to observe other conditions like a curfew restricting the hours they could go out at night. The Tracking Scheme could thus help to reduce short-term care and at the same time begin to work with young people who might be placed with it. All those young people remanded into care or custody in the first nine months of the Scheme's operation were referred.

The development of the Tracking Scheme was jointly managed by Neil Morgan, the Director of the Chichester Diocesan Association, Barry Anderson, then Intermediate Treatment Officer of West Sussex County Council, and Richard Munnion for the Probation Service. They represented three of the agencies on the Western Division Intermediate Treatment Committee which had supported the application to the DHSS for funds under the LAC(83)3 initiative, the others being the education and youth services, the police, the magistrates and the magistrates' clerks. The project staff did not use outside consultants on a regular basis but sometimes employed other workers in Intermediate Treatment for sessions. They held weekly staff meetings for sharing information and problems. The Project Leader supervised the staff, developing training to meet the needs of each individual, and was responsible to the three managers. A staff development programme included performance appraisal sessions and working with colleagues on projects to learn their particular areas of expertise. To pay for equipment like one fibre-glass and one wooden boat, gardening tools and a 35 millimetre camera, the Scheme obtained grants from local trusts and the IT Fund.

The impact of the scheme

There is no doubt about the impact of the West Sussex Tracking Scheme on the young offenders who were sent to it, or that they might have been sent into custody if it had not been for the Scheme. The problem about the Scheme, which in the end contributed to its extinction, was that it served so few. In the 18 months from its start until July 1986 it had only 19 young people on programmes. The reason for the small number was not so much that the courts still preferred custody. Figures prepared by John Gibson, the Assistant Project Leader, showed that the number sent into custody in the period by the relevant courts was reduced to six, two of whom had re-offended whilst on the Tracking Scheme, the other four having committed violent crimes or arson. The length of time juveniles spent in custody during the 18 months was a third of that spent in custody by juveniles during 1984. The trouble was that the Scheme had been set up to serve only one of the three divisions of West Sussex: the catchment area was too small to supply more young people without drawing in those who were not really at risk of custody or care.

Here are two examples of the kind of young people on the Scheme, showing a pattern of persistent offending.

Billy

Age	Court Appearances	Offences	Disposals
12	1	Theft	Supervision Order
	2	Theft	Care Order S 7.7
		Burglary	
		Deception	
13	3	Receiving	Fine
	4	Theft, TWOC	Sentence Deferred

14	5	TWOC	120 Days DC
	6	Attempting to drive away a vehicle	Conditional Discharge
	7	TWOC	Conditional Discharge
	8	Criminal Damage TWOC	Secure Accommodation Order
15	9	TDA × 3 Criminal Damage Breaking & entering	2 year SO with Tracking

TWOC Taking a car Without Owner's Consent
TDA Taking and Driving Away a car
DC Detention Centre
ACO Attendance Centre Order
SO Supervision Order

Billy successfully completed his programme without re-offending. He was returned to court for offences connected with his ninth appearance and the court made a two-year Supervision Order to run concurrently with the one already made. It appears that Billy had experienced a taste of most disposals, from Supervision early on, to Detention Centre at 14, and had been kept in secure accommodation at one stage (though this could not have been a disposal for his offences), before he was sent to the Tracking Scheme.

Jimmy

Age	Court Appearance	Offences	Disposals
14	1	Burglary/Theft × 2	24 hours ACO
	2	Theft, Handling	2-year SO with IT
	3	Burglary Theft × 2 Deception × 4	SO discharged DC 1 month
15	4	Burlgary and theft × 2 Burglary and theft with others Theft	Care Order S 7.7
	5	Criminal Damage Allowed self to be carried	DC 3 months DC 3 months concurrent
	6	Burglary and theft with others	DC 30 days for all offences

130

		TWOC	concurrent
		Burglary and theft	
16	7	Criminal Damage	Deferred sentence
		Burglary	
	8	Burglary × 3	Youth Custody 125 days
		Criminal Damage	30 days concurrent
	9	Criminal Damage	CD 2 years on each
		Burglary	
	10	Burglary × 3	SO 2 years with tracking

Jimmy's first punishment was an Attendance Centre Order. Detention Centres, to which he was sent regularly from the age of 14, seemed to do little to affect his pattern of behaviour. His programme on the Tracking Scheme broke down after 76 days and he was sent into youth custody for 12 months for two burglaries, a theft, deception and criminal damage. He spent over one year and nine months of his first 17 years in custody.

Both examples, which the workers described as typical rather than extreme, show that there were persistent offenders in the Western area for the Tracking Scheme to work with, but it is difficult to make many generalizations from a total of 19 cases in 18 months. However, all the young people were white in an area where there were few from ethnic minorities. All were male except for one girl towards the end of the Scheme who had been involved in burglaries with an adult, was sniffing glue and drinking, although under age. She was on the Scheme as an alternative to care as well as custody.

All but one had been sent to the Scheme after recommendations in a court report. Altogether, there were 47 referrals to the Scheme for assessment in the 17 months from February 1985 to July 1986. There were 21 other non-custodial disposals, described as 'lower in the tariff'. Of the 19 young people on the Scheme, nine had to be taken back to court for breaches of their orders and all were fined and returned to the Scheme. Four re-offended whilst on the Scheme and all but Jimmy were returned to the Scheme to complete their programmes. Jimmy was the only offender not to stay the course. After completing their time on the Scheme, however, seven were reconvicted for offences in the period reviewed, three of whom then went into custody.

Platten's report on the period concluded that the Tracking Scheme changed the sentencing patterns in the Western area by giving the magistrates an alternative they lacked before. Those given custody once the Scheme was in operation had committed more serious offences than many of those sent into custody in the previous year. Custody remained

131

the preferred option for the most serious offenders, especially those who had used violence. It is always difficult to compare rates of recidivism and particularly so when the number of cases is small, but the report points out that the Scheme's recidivism rate for those reconvicted whilst on programmes was 36 per cent, similar to the US figure quoted by Jerome Miller for recidivism in Massachusetts when custodial institutions throughout the state were closed.

The demise of the scheme

In October 1986, when the DHSS grant was about to finish and a decision had still not been made about the Scheme's future by the agencies concerned in West Sussex, John Platten prepared several papers for the Intermediate Treatment Review which was looking at the Scheme in relation to the general provision of Intermediate Treatment in West Sussex. In particular he compared the figures available for the Western Division and its Tracking Scheme with those for the Specified Activities Scheme run in the Worthing area. The programme for specified activities had been available since soon after the implementation of the Criminal Justice Act 1982. It was designed as an alternative to custody and care for 14 to 16 year olds as a condition of a Supervision Order.

The young people concerned came from the Petty Session Divisions of Arundel, Worthing and Steyning. A similar scheme existed in Crawley for those from the Mid-Sussex, Horsham and Crawley Divisions. The young people attended the scheme for 100 hours which were followed by a period of supervision by a probation officer or social worker in their home area. There was a firm policy of returning to court any young person who failed to comply with the agreed conditions. Before the disposal was made magistrates and judges were asked to remand the young offenders on bail for three or four weeks to enable consultation with all concerned to produce an outline of the proposed programme for the court to consider. (The idea of such a remand assessment period, also used in Kirklees, had been rejected by the Tracking Scheme, as it was felt that it might extend the young person's sentence without guaranteeing a place on the Scheme at the end of the month's assessment.)

The programme was similar to that offered by the Tracking Scheme but without the intensive tracking element. Designed to be 'sufficiently flexible to meet the needs of different groups and take into account individual need', it lasted eight weeks for each participant with a short residential period at Knowles Tooth Children's Centre. It encompassed 'basic formal education and creative activity; an examination of offending behaviour; life and social skills in dealing with relationships, personal competence, work, leisure and alcohol; practical skills and service to society'. The methods used were individual counselling and groupwork, including discussion, role-play, work with videos, games and practical tasks enabling group members to learn by experience. The centres at Worthing and Crawley each had the services of one full-time probation officer, a qualified part-time teacher, sessional supervisors and voluntary associates.

The comparison made was between the first 47 young people referred to each of the schemes, between 1 October 1983 and 11 March 1986 for the Specified Activities Scheme, and 7 January 1985 and 21 May 1986 for the Tracking Scheme. The percentage who ended in custody was greater among those referred in the Worthing area, 19 per cent compared with 10 per cent, but as the details of the cases are not given it is hard to draw any conclusions about the reasons for the difference. However, the Tracking Scheme was able to consider all the young people at risk of custody or care in its area, whereas in the Worthing area 19 others were sent into custody in addition to those whom the Specified Activities Scheme had considered.

In general, as alternatives to custody and care were developed in all three areas, so the number of Supervision Orders increased. After the introduction of the Tracking Scheme in the Western area, no Care Orders for criminal matters were made there. The number was reduced but they were not eliminated in the other two areas. The Platten paper estimated that it cost West Sussex County Council between £94,000 and £196,000 to maintain in local authority residential establishments the seven young people given Care Orders during 1985 in the other two areas which did not have the alternatives to care offered by the Western area.

The Tracking Scheme could therefore be shown to have been effective in offering alternatives to custody and care in an area which previously has used custody and care for criminal matters extensively. The rate at which those who attended the Scheme had re-offended was certainly lower than the national average for re-offending after a custodial sentence, and the Scheme was approved by local magistrates, by supervising officers and by the families involved. An independent researcher had interviewed parents whose sons had completed programmes in the Scheme's first year. Their comments were of the tenor: 'It altered our attitude on how to handle him. We were able to copy and carry on from the Scheme', and 'He grew up while on the Scheme through having a friend'.

In making the case for the continuation of the Scheme as early as the end of the first year, John Platten had asked, and answered in the affirmative, questions used to evaluate the Medway Close Support Unit in Kent and reported in the Home Office's *Research Bulletin* No. 16. Did the need for such a project exist locally? The answer was clearly 'yes'. Did the programme of planned activities actually take place, and how continuously was it available? One hundred per cent scoring here. Did the courts make use of the project? We have seen that they did. Did the project manage to attract its intended target group – those who otherwise would have been sent into custody? Yes. Was control of the project adequate? How well was attendance at the project secured? How was control kept within the project programme? How well did the project contain the offence behaviour of those passing through it? These questions could all be adequately answered. What was the re-offending rate of those passing through the programmes? Some re-offended but not all, and not with such dire results as might otherwise have been the case. Finally, what were the costs of the project compared with the costs of custody?

The financial issue was to be decisive for the future of the Scheme. The annual expenditure on the Tracking Scheme was £55,000, the amount of the grant received from the DHSS. Those costs did not include what the local authority spent for the time of their social workers who held the Supervision Orders and liaised with the trackers. The daily costs of delivering the programmes could be said, however, to be approximately £144. Depending on how many young people at any one time were on the Scheme (between four and eight during 1985) the cost was between £36 and £52 a day for each young person. This compared with daily costs in a Detention Centre of £47, in closed youth custody of £37 and open youth custody of £42. On average the Scheme cost less. However, the saving was not to the local authority but to the Home Office which financed custodial provision.

It was also argued that the Scheme was marginally cheaper for the local authority than having young people in residential establishments, although the paper which in December 1986 recommended that the Western Division should merge with the Southern concluded that the costs were 'comparable'. The paper commented that 'Many representations have been made about the success of this Scheme, though few people are aware of the resources committed to it.' The crucial point was that the workload in the Western Division was less than in the other two, yet the provision was higher.

In December 1986 the Social Services Committee decided that it was not prepared to take over the DHSS funding of £55,000 a year to continue the Tracking Scheme. Instead, there would be a common scheme for Intermediate Treatment throughout the county, operating from two bases and organized jointly by probation and social services. The North Eastern Division would be covered from the probation premises in Crawley, the other, combining the Western and Southern Divisions, would be in the Social Services' premises in Littlehampton. There would be an overall manager for the county appointed by the Social Services Department. The scheme would be managed on a day-to-day basis by Social Services but under overall joint management by social services and probation.

What was to happen to the concept of tracking? The paper agreed by the Social Services Committee explained: 'It is felt that the benefits of the tracking system for some children should certainly be made available across the county, and it is proposed that sessional supervisors should be used for this kind of activity particularly when intensive supervision is necessary. The existing staff are all on limited term contracts to the Chichester Diocesan Association for Family Social Work and it is proposed to allow them access to probation and social services vacancies as if they were internal candidates.'

With the end, after a long period of uncertainty, of their independent project of which tracking had been the main feature, the staff in fact dispersed. In spite of the undertaking to allow them access to vacancies as if they were internal candidates, the fact that none of them had social work qualifications went against them and their experience was not counted as equivalent. They were eligible only for Assistant Social Worker posts. John Platten became a Lecturer in Community and Youth Studies at St Martin's College, Lancaster, one member of the team changed to youth work while doing some sessions of Intermediate Treatment, one went to work with the long-term unemployed, one to take a sports studies course and one moved to East Anglia. None had been offered an assured job with West Sussex and as a result the expertise they had built up as a team for the two-year period was lost.

Their experience underlines the hazards of working in Intermediate Treatment schemes which are experimental projects rather than elements in an area's strategy for young people. Can a service have the highest professional standards if it employs key staff on a short-term basis and does not offer them opportunities for their careers? Should there be a separate career structure (and a distinct qualification) for those who specialize in Intermediate Treatment? Would such separation overcome the difficulty of there not being parity of pay and conditions for those coming from the different professions of social work, education and youth and community work? These are questions which must be addressed in order to make the most of the skills of those already working in this field.

The factors that led to the closure of the Scheme were built into it from the start. First, the small number of young people needing alternatives to custody or care in the Western area made the cost *per capita* of such intensive, one-to-one supervision comparatively high. Second, the financial arrangement with the probation service was crucial, difficult to break since through it the area received substantial extra funding from the Home Office. However, the outcome of the experiment in the Western Division could have been the replication of the tracking element throughout West Sussex. There are logistical difficulties in having a single tracking scheme for so big a geographical area but tracking could have been part of each Division's plan for those given Supervision Orders with specified activities. As it was, the central pillar of the Western scheme, the tracking, was pared down into a peripheral support, to be available sometimes as an extra. The opportunity to use the funding offered by the DHSS initiative must have been tempting but it is hard to see how the applicants convinced the funders that West Sussex planned to integrate a tracking scheme into its general provision.

Key features

The key features of the West Sussex Tracking Scheme are clear with regard to its practice with young offenders. Its organizational framework was complicated but what happened to the Scheme can be summarized.

- Intensive contact by the trackers, with the investment of time ensuring a close relationship.
- Close involvement of families.
- Regular use of residential courses as part of the programmes.
- A Bail Condition Support Scheme subsequently developed.
- Staff not social workers but from youth and community work.
- Frequent reporting back to magistrates, good links with social workers and probation officers and emphasis on public relations.

• Clearly aimed at those at risk of custody or care and successful in offering an alternative for those whose offences did not involve violence.

• The Scheme covered only one of three local authority Divisions and was slotted into an existing system.

• Small potential pool of clients in the Division for an alternative to custody and care project.

• No central monitoring of the juvenile justice system but monitoring of performance by the Scheme itself.

• The Scheme was not continued after its initial two years as the local authority Social Services Department was unwilling to take on the financial commitment for a separate tracking scheme in one area or to recast Intermediate Treatment throughout West Sussex in a way that radically changed the existing arrangements with the Probation Service.

6

Non-Statutory Intervention
Project Centres in Berkshire

The Royal County of Berkshire Social Services Department has six Divisions, each of which had a project centre for young people established before the 1982 Criminal Justice Act. In addition there are two projects which are alternatives to custody or care, one in Reading (developed in association with the Community Projects Foundation and founded with DHSS support in June 1983) and the other in Slough, set up under the DHSS 1983 initiative. The tradition in Berkshire had been for each Division to have a considerable degree of autonomy and to develop its services according to local needs. There have accordingly been different ways of presenting services for young people and some areas concentrated more than others on developing Intermediate Treatment. In 1983, however, after a review of residential services for children, several children's homes were closed. The substantial annual revenue and some of the buildings thus freed were allocated to the centres. These continued to develop on individual lines until in 1986 a common staff structure was introduced. An organizer, deputy organizer and two workers, with clerical support, were established in each Division and a framework agreed for the development of practice and procedure at all the centres.

The consistent feature of all the centres has been that they have served not only juvenile offenders on court orders but also children who from a comparatively young age have been identified as likely to offend or need care in future. Thus the handbook of the St Mary's Project Centre at Maidenhead, published in June 1987, begins 'It is some ten years since the name St Mary's was linked with a new community service for children and young people who were "at risk", likely to offend, or who had appeared before the juvenile court.' Similarly the Slough Project Centre, 'Transit', gives as its primary objectives:

(a) To provide a range of community based activities, known as Intermediate Treatment which will be made available to the Slough Juvenile Court.

(b) To provide a range of supportive services to children and young people who may be at risk of coming before courts or being admitted to care.

In addition, Transit hopes to provide programmes which can assist young people in leaving care, to contribute to community assessment programmes, to provide information and facilities for other agencies and groups in the Division (for example for social inquiry reports) and to be involved in the development of work with young people both in the community and in residential care. Since the end of 1986 these have been the primary and additional aims of all the centres, as laid down in operational guidelines agreed for the centres and published in August 1986.

The six Social Services Divisions with centres, are Bracknell, Newbury, Reading, Slough, Windsor/Maidenhead and Wokingham, the two big towns having as well as their centres the projects which are solely alternatives to custody or care. Close co-operation between the Social Services Department and the Probation Service is fundamental to the planning of services and the Berkshire Youth Projects Trust has also been established to develop further facilities. Four of the centres are in detached houses which used to be children's homes, one of them sharing the premises with an educational withdrawal unit; the fifth, in Maidenhead, occupies the top floor of a former fire station and the sixth is in a building acquired from the Education Department. All have equipment like computers and videos, facilities for photography and artwork, but few have space outdoors for more than limited activities. By the end of 1986 five of the centres had a minibus for transporting children from and to their homes, for day trips and residential periods.

Since 1983 the department has begun to monitor what happens to young offenders in Berkshire and some of their characteristics. The number of children of primary school age in the population was decreasing until 1984 but is now expected to rise until 1990, with a corresponding decrease in the number of 11 to 16 year-olds until 1990, especially in urban areas. It is estimated that in 1990 there will be at least 25 per cent fewer secondary school children than there were in 1981. This population change, with an increase in cautioning of juveniles by Thames Valley police, on the lines advocated by the 1985 Home Office circular, has reduced the number of young people coming before the courts.

In a report to the Social Services Committee, published in September 1987 (*Criminal Justice Act 1982 – Four Years On*) Tom Butler, Service Development Officer, showed that between 1983 and 1987 there was a reduction of 40 per cent in the number of social inquiry reports prepared for the juvenile courts, from 456 for the year ending May, 1984, to 274 for the year ending May, 1987. Probation completed more than three quarters of the reports, reflecting the fact that 80 per cent of the young people were over 15 years of age. Between June 1986 and June 1987, a third of the 274 cases for which reports were prepared were for theft or handling stolen goods and over a quarter were for burglary. There was a slight increase over previous years in the number of cases involving violence, rising to 14 per cent of the total. The number sent to a detention centre went down from 42 in 1983/84 to 18 in 1986/87, sent to youth custody from nine to five, and sent into care in criminal proceedings, from 20 to four. These reductions reflect the availability and growing acceptability of the alternatives to custody. Almost half of the custodial orders in 1986/87 were made in Reading, more than a quarter in Slough, four of the 18 given custodial sentences were first offenders, and a further six had only one previous finding of guilt. It is interesting to note that more Supervision Orders with conditions of Intermediate Treatment were made than were recommended in the reports.

There are no overall figures about the number and types of young people attending centres in the county on a voluntary basis. As in many social services departments, central monitoring systems have not been a priority but in 1988 it was agreed in the department's three-year plan for children's services to establish a system for monitoring the work of the project centres. Ten per cent of the population of Reading are of Afro-Caribbean or Asian origin and the Granville Road Project, the alternative to custody project in Reading, was from the start conscious of the needs of black young people, recruiting two black workers. However, it is not council policy to carry out ethnic monitoring so information is not available which might be helpful to this and other projects in planning appropriate provision.

The individual centres, however, can give information about the children and young people with whom they work. Between April 1987 and March 1988, St Mary's worked with 112 young people, only six of whom were on court orders, and the Transit Centre at Slough serves over 150 young people a year. On 1 February 1988 the Transit Centre had 25 children currently referred aged between seven and 11 and 30 young people aged 12 to 17. Thus the first distinctive feature of a project which offers a broad approach is the younger age of many of the children with whom preventive work is undertaken. The second is the number of girls involved. In Surrey at the Juvenile Offender Resource Centre, in Lambeth at the Junction Project and on the West Sussex Tracking Scheme, hardly a single girl appeared, but here in Slough there were seven girls under 12 and ten aged 12 to 17. The referrals for both age groups came mainly from the social services but some came from schools and child guidance clinics and one from a children's home. Only six were on Supervision Orders with an Intermediate Treatment requirement and most were referred through family problems rather than because they were thought to be specifically at risk of offending.

As only a minority of those attending the Transit Centre had at that time been sent by the courts, it might be supposed that young people attend the six centres in Berkshire at will and for unspecified periods. This is not the case. Programmes are drawn up for each child or young person referred, with set objectives and for a set length of time with reviews and evaluation of the work undertaken regularly. There are signed agreements between all concerned which are sometimes called contracts. The centres are not youth clubs run by social services, even if some of the activities are the same as those in youth clubs. They offer structured, time-limited intervention in the lives of the young people and their families, aiming to fit the young people into facilities in the community afterwards. In many ways they are more similar than different to the projects already described which are alternatives to custody or care for serious offenders.

We have seen that it is impossible to separate the welfare element from the other work that goes on in a project for juvenile offenders. It is an integral part of work with any young offender to address his or her welfare. In the projects which are alternatives to custody or care, however, the presenting problem is different and this naturally affects their focus and ethos. What brought the young person to the project was a court appearance for a serious offence. Custody or care were the alternatives to attending the project. By contrast, custody and care are only on the horizon for those who attend centres on a voluntary basis or for those who are on court orders but not at present at risk of being removed from home. There will therefore be less emphasis in these projects on analysing offending behaviour, although it will be included for those who need it. The emphasis is more on improving general skills and helping young people to develop their potential and to understand the choices they can make.

The handbook for St Mary's states its philosophy at the outset: 'The philosophy of St Mary's reflects a belief in the capacity of young people to grow towards achieving their full potential. It believes that in the right conditions that potential can be developed. It believes that young people have the right, and the ability, to make their own decisions about their lives.' St Mary's translates this philosophy into an aim to create an environment which:

(a) assists young people in understanding themselves and their environment

(b) assists young people in taking responsibility for their actions and recognising the consequences of them

(c) assists young people in acknowledging and understanding the limitations which constrain individuals in their response to society and to structural inequalities and injustices therein, which may be contributing to the young person's problems.

The young people who frequently find their way to residential care or appear before the courts are those, in its view, who have not found the support they need through their families, friends or any 'significant others'.

The work at St Mary's begins with individual assessment of a young person's needs. Referrals come from social services, probation, child guidance, the Education Welfare Service or other agencies. They may be made direct to the centre or through the Divisional Office. Those who make the referrals are asked to specify the factors which in their view make the young person 'at risk' in both the long and short term. The short-term needs are those which have probably precipitated the referral. Perhaps the boy or girl needs immediate help to prevent exclusion from school. But the programme must also consider how the young person reached the position of nearly being excluded and what long-term changes can prevent the same situation arising again.

A considerable amount of information is required on the referral form which each project incorporates in the referral system it has developed. At St Mary's, as well as details of all members of the young person's household, their GP's name is required and any relevant medical information, a contact at school and details of involvement with any other agencies. Before completing the form those who make referrals have to be sure that the help they are seeking from St Mary's is not already available elsewhere, for example at a local youth club. They have to be able to answer 'What are your plans and aims in working with the young person and his/her family?', and have sufficient knowledge of the young person to explain how they currently use their spare time. They cannot expect to hand the problem, as it were, to St Mary's and leave it to St Mary's to solve. They will be involved throughout, usually doing whatever work is necessary with the family, and retaining responsibility. In addition, they must be open with the young person and the family since all the information on the form may be shared with them by the Centre unless the worker making the referral arranges to the contrary. The teams at the project centres decide on the basis of the information given whether or not to accept referrals.

Like the projects which are alternatives to custody and care, the centres use, as appropriate, individual work, group work, residential sessions and work with families. On individual work, the St Mary's handbook explains that the worker may join the young person on a one-to-one basis in an activity they can undertake together, whether a craft, a sport or a hobby, in order to develop a trusting relationship. Secondly, he or she will help the young person to discover clubs and groups in the community to join or activities to pursue.

The groups at the centres are based on common needs. For example, there will usually be one on offending behaviour for those who have been in trouble, one for those with difficulties at school and general groups to improve social skills and family relationships. The Transit Centre at Slough explains that groupwork has distinct benefits for clients, workers and the agencies, reducing isolation for everyone and encouraging everyone to help each other. As a general objective the groups aim:

1   To enable the development of self-esteem.
2   To look at self-awareness and relationships with others, with authority and with families.
3   To provide the opportunity to express feelings.
4   To point out the consequences of actions, allow insight into behaviour and the effect it has on others.

As far as offenders are concerned, the aim is to identify in what situations offending occurs and why; to consider other choices that may be available when faced with the opportunity and/or pressure to offend; to consider how offending affects the offender and his/her victim; to consider what happens if a decision is made to re-offend; to understand and accept that each person is responsible for his or her own behaviour.

A specimen programme for a group on offending behaviour at St Mary's covers 12 sessions. Those in the group begin by writing together a scenario about an actual offence that took place one evening. They then act out their script and record this on video. In the next session they discuss, act out and record other ways in which the story might have developed or ended. On the third evening they use the script to look at how choices are made. In the two following sessions they watch a video which raises issues about why people break the law. They go on to use role-play, discussion and other activities to explore the consequences of their court appearances, consider the views of magistrates and neighbours and the effect on their future employment. The final sessions look at other ways of using spare time and the consequences of re-offending. The budget for a group of this kind meeting once a week for 12 weeks was £56 in 1987 which covered refreshments at the centre and outside, the hire of videos and an excursion.

Short, residential periods are built into the programmes of most young people. The projects go to a small, country centre just outside Reading and adventure centres in Wales for outdoor activities like camping, rock climbing, orienteering and abseiling. They find spells away from base helpful for getting to know the young people well and can use the dynamics of the group constructively, showing the participants what they can offer each other.

Most work with families is done by the worker who referred the young person but parents are encouraged to attend meetings and reviews, to participate in drawing up the programme and to sign the contract or agreement. There is also sometimes, at Transit for example, a group for parents to meet each other and look at ways they can be helped to reduce their children's risk of offending or entering care.

In general, the centres are open during the day but most of the work in the school term with children of school age takes place in the early evenings and at weekends. The Transit Centre in Slough had a Junior Scheme in early 1988 with 15 children aged from seven to 11. These were mainly children who were at risk within their families and often were on the child abuse register. They attended the centre for only one evening a week for three hours during term but there were extensive holiday programmes for them at Easter and in the summer when they needed care most.

The 'contract' for the programme at St Mary's is in many ways similar to those used in projects where young people all attend under court orders. A single document is signed by all the parties (young person, parent, referrer and St Mary's). It begins by giving the aims of the programme and then states what the programme will be, continuing:

> 'In accepting the programme . . . agrees to keep to the times agreed and fulfil the following conditions:. . . . (Parent). . . . agrees to ensure . . . 's regular attendance and to participate in the programme and review by arrangement.'

A date for the review of the programme/contract is given at the end. The main difference between this agreement and ones used in projects which are alternatives to custody or care is that there is no clause explaining the sanctions if the rules are broken.

Workers say that by signing the contract parents acknowledge that there is a problem to be tackled and that is why their child is attending the centre. They are not worried by the fact that their child may not have been in trouble with the law, whereas others have been sent to the centre by the courts, since they recognize the need for intervention and want help. The idea that their child may be 'infected' by young delinquents, as is said to happen when young offenders are locked up together, either does not occur to them or is sensibly discounted because of the circumstances and their trust in the centre.

St Mary's also has a Health and Consent Form for the parents to complete giving details of illnesses, allergies, any medication, tetanus inoculation, whether the child suffers from travel sickness, can swim or wets the bed. The 'consent' part of the form states:

> I . . . give my consent for . . . to attend the Project and take part in the various activities and outings arranged. If my child should require emergency medical treatment I give my consent for the necessary treatment to be carried out. I also give consent for any photographs taken for the group to be shared with other group members. I understand that Berkshire County Council or its staff cannot be held responsible for any loss of property.

Volunteers

The six project centres in Berkshire have been developed as resources for their local communities. It is consistent with the principles on which the Berkshire strategy is based that the projects should encourage volunteers from the community to join professional workers in developing programmes for young people. They explain at St Mary's that the use of volunteers, sessional workers and Community Service Volunteers helps provide a better and wider range of services for young people.

The volunteers are used to help run groups and to befriend young people on an individual basis. All have to undergo for selection interviews and training weekends at which they must demonstrate their potential to achieve the tasks involved. They come from a wide variety of backgrounds. Some are personal friends of staff, others work in different kinds of social, youth work and teaching, or have been enlisted through local volunteer bureaux. There are checks of references and police records before they are taken on and they are given regular supervision and training. Only out-of-pocket expenses are paid yet at any one time each project attracts an average of five to ten volunteers, willing and able to give young people the benefit of their time and skills.

This is the kind of involvement and commitment from the community which bodies like the Personal Social Services Council in its 1977 report *A Future for Intermediate Treatment* advocated. Numbers of volunteers fluctuate and depend very much on the energy and time staff make available to train and support them. When such efforts are made, the volunteers provide a rich source of support to young people both within and outside the project centres.

Those volunteers who have particular skills, perhaps in a craft, sport or computing, or who are thought able on their own to carry the responsibility, for example, of co-ordinating a group, may as sessional workers be paid a fee dependent on qualifications and experience. Other sessional workers are recruited to provide special instruction, including teachers for groups set up to tackle problems relating to school. Community Service Volunteers are used in a similar way to ordinary volunteers but on a full-time basis.

Social inquiry reports

All the project centres have, as part of their general brief, a duty to contribute to community assessment programmes and to provide information for social inquiry reports and recommendations. At the Transit Centre in Slough a panel to consider social inquiry reports meets each week, consisting of the Project Centre organizer, who is the officer from the project who attends court, the leader of the Slough Direct Alternative to Custody Project, two social workers from the Social Services Department and a juvenile specialist from the Probation Department.

The purpose of the panel is to aid consistency between the agencies in writing reports and to provide information and consultation on the various options open to courts for the writers of reports to consider when making recommendations. The panel has the following principles in mind:

1 The material contained in the report should be relevant to the young person's offending or to his likely response to the various options of the court.
2 All recommendations should be for the minimum amount of intervention in the young person's life in view of his offending behaviour.
3 That non-custodial alternatives should be considered whenever relevant, with constructive alternatives to custody put forward wherever possible.

The Transit Centre's guidelines are designed 'to ensure that no inappropriate recommendations from social services go before the Court'. Although there is firm emphasis on the minimum of intervention, and on alternatives to custody, these guidelines by implication do not rule out that custody may sometimes be inevitable for certain crimes or offenders. In some local authorities it is departmental policy never to make a recommendation for custody. It is argued that custody can only be justified on judicial grounds and therefore it is a measure to be contemplated only by magistrates or judges. The writers of reports are advised not to make a recommendation at all if they cannot make a case for an alternative to custody. However, it would seem more logical and constructive to continue to put the case for more work in the community than to abrogate all responsibility.

It can be seen that the Transit Centre in Slough offers a broad range of services, from programmes for young offenders on orders with requirements for Intermediate Treatment, to reports to the courts on young offenders, to the Junior Scheme described previously for children at risk through no fault of their own. Another role of this centre for those at risk of offending is in offering advice and help to parents of young people who have been cautioned. It is normal practice for the police to notify social services and other relevant agencies of any involvement with juveniles. The Centre responds to all new notifications and arranges meetings through the Community Liaison Division between the policy community liaison officers and other interested agencies. It also tries to encourage the repeated use of cautions by the police, particularly for those young people with whom social services or other agencies are already working.

From the aspect of care, the Transit Centre is committed to help those children who are already placed away from home by the local authority. It provides opportunities for young people to attend projects in the community away from the confines of residential homes; help in supporting placements which run into difficulties; help in ensuring that residential placements do not last longer than necessary; and help in supporting young people who come from Slough so that they do not have to leave their home area.

Evaluation

It is hard enough to agree on criteria for evaluating the effectiveness of projects which are alternatives to custody or care, so can there be any consensus about criteria for projects with a broader approach and with different kinds of children and young people attending? The operational guidelines Berkshire adopted in 1986 have a section called 'Success Criteria'. In general, it says, attention should be paid to the number of young people referred, the number accepted within pre-established criteria, and the number completing the programme. A division is then made between 'Intermediate Treatment Programmes' and 'Individual Goals'.

As might be expected, the criteria of success for those on Intermediate Treatment programmes include the number who complete the programme without re-offending, or without re-offending within a year, or whose rate of offending is reduced. They also entail examining the number ordered into custody or care by the courts as a proportion of those who appear before the courts and compared with previous years. Each project centre should therefore keep accurate records of those attending on court orders. Reviews involve the parents and the supervisor with responsibility for the order, as well as the young person and project centre staff. They are held at least half-way through an Intermediate Treatment programme and at the end.

Individual development and growth would be impossible to monitor in the short term if the goals were not specific. The projects may aim for general improvement in areas like relationships with the family and peer groups, but the objectives agreed in the contracts are usually broken down in detail. A child who is a truant from school may have as one of his or her aims to get up each morning at a set time and reach school before the register is marked. Improved attendance and behaviour at school can be charted with the school's co-operation and the child's efforts encouraged. Relationships in the family can be improved if reasonable rules are agreed, like 'to tell my Mum when I'm going out and when I'll be back'.

At St Mary's they evaluate the work of the Centre as a whole in an annual review which looks back over the previous year and plans the one ahead. A review is held on each young person every three months and all work is recorded and supervised. For work on an individual basis all significant contact with the young person, the family and any agency involved is recorded and examined during normal staff supervision sessions. Before a group begins its aims, the programme and the methods to be used are stated. As soon as possible after each session the supervisor meets the leaders to consider:

Were the aims for the session met?
Were the methods chosen the most productive?
Did the session help in achieving the group's aims?
Is the group helping to achieve the individual aims for its members?
Is the programme for the next session still appropriate?
What preparation is necessary for the next session? Who will do it?
Did the working of the leaders help or hinder the group in any way?

Any information relevant to individual young people is extracted and entered into their files. As has been seen, a budget is made for each group and at the end of the group it is considered whether the money was spent as effectively as possible.

The staff of the project centres are nearly all qualified in social work, teaching or youth and community work but experienced staff who do not have formal qualifications are eligible for the post of project worker. They are paid on local authority National Joint Council rather than social work scales, to accommodate different professional backgrounds. The budget for the financial year 1988–89 for the six centres was just under half a million pounds. One project centre calculated that the cost for each child served by the centre was approximately £600.

The project centres are seen as an integral part of the Children and Families Group within each of Berkshire's six Divisions. The organizers of the centres are responsible to the Assistant Divisional Director for Children and Families and as part of their remit have to liaise with other local agencies and magistrates. Close relationships with schools in their patch are obviously essential to identify those children who need preventive help and with voluntary agencies who may be helping families generally. Although separate from each other, the centres often work together and share facilities. Local Intermediate Treatment Development Groups were in 1988 being replaced by Juvenile Justice Advisory Groups to cover all aspects of work with young offenders.

At the end of 1986 there was a proposal to introduce specialist juvenile justice teams, consisting of social workers, probation officers and Centre staff, to provide a pre-court information service, social inquiry reports, supervisors for those given Supervision Orders and possible for those given Community Service Orders or released after custody. The proposal was not adopted, however, because of the reduction in the number of cases coming to court and the reduction in the use of custody. The Social Services and Probation Committees decided that in the circumstances such a change could not be justified. In 1988 it was agreed instead to build on the existing framework and base the Social Services Department's provision for young offenders at the project centres, with a member of the field work staff in some Divisions also specializing in work with offenders as necessary.

The effect of this change on the work of the centres was not expected to be great since the number of offenders involved was so small. However, it would mean to some extent a greater concentration on work with offenders, particularly those at risk of custody or care in areas where there was no specialist centre for them, and a corresponding reduction in the time spent on young people on the edges of delinquency. It was hoped that good contacts between social services and community groups would ensure that the needs of younger children were adequately met. Holiday play schemes, for example, could be run by the District Council Leisure and Amenities Departments in all areas. It was agreed to establish a County Standing Conference on Young Offenders with prevention as part of its remit, consisting of representatives from social services, probation, education, the police, the Crown Prosecution Service, magistrates, justices' clerks, the juvenile justice advisory groups, voluntary organizations and local community groups. The tasks of the centres were listed as:

> to contribute to joint agency or similar arrangements for decisions on cautioning;
> to provide social inquiry reports;
> to provide supervisory officers for those on Supervision Orders;

to supervise licence requirements for juveniles subject to Detention Centre or Youth Custody Orders;

to provide an officer in court to advise magistrates, present school reports and advise other staff as necessary;

to contribute to the development of crime prevention measures;

to promote the joint policy of the social work and probation agencies in relation to young offenders through the provision of information about facilities and liaison with local agencies and individuals;

to contribute to arrangements for monitoring and evaluating services.

The staff providing the services would consist of probation officers as well as the centre staff and specialist fieldworkers if necessary. The boundaries of the court Petty Sessional Divisions and the agencies concerned did not coincide but it was hoped that local knowledge would overcome difficulties. A small group of senior officers from both agencies would form a Joint Agency Forum to assist in implementing the policy, to develop systems for monitoring practice and evaluating outcomes, to arrange meetings and resolve difficulties. As before, the emphasis was on using facilities in the community before those provided by the centres.

Key features

This description of the six project centres in Berkshire has shown that they have many similar features to projects which are alternatives to custody. The aims for the individual young people who attend the centres are clearly defined and the intervention is for a specific purpose. What we do not know at the moment, partly because statistical information is not available, is the effect of intervention at an early stage on offending behaviour or the risk of entering care.

It is sometimes argued that if young people are drawn into the ambit of social services before it is essential, they are labelled as likely delinquents. Social workers may connive in such labelling by not recommending Intermediate Treatment for those who have attended schemes if they subsequently offend, on the grounds that work in the community has been tried. They may believe that magistrates who read in court reports that young people have attended projects on a voluntary basis will be reluctant to order Intermediate Treatment. They should try to persuade them by arguing the appropriateness of the programme and the need to repeat the lesson. However, it is only possible to speculate about the extent to which such labelling of young people takes place and affects them adversely. There is far too little research into the reasons for court disposals or the effects of social work intervention but the available statistics from Berkshire and the impressions of workers do not support such fears. Good communication between social services, probation and the courts is clearly essential to avoid the danger of preventive services rebounding on young people.

The key features of the project centres in Berkshire can be summarized in the following points:

• They are part of a strategy for the county, within the Children and Families sector, consisting of two projects which are alternatives to custody or care and the six centres. The centres are broadly based, for both young offenders and for those at risk of becoming offenders or being taken into care because of the breakdown of their families.

• There is close co-operation with probation in a joint policy on juvenile offenders, and with the police over cautioning and helping families of young people who are cautioned.

• The six centres are locally based and deal as much with school and family problems as offending.

• Younger children and more girls attend than at projects which are only alternatives to custody.

• Those sent by the courts to the broadly-based centres may include some on 90-day programmes as an alternative to custody and others on 60-day or 30-day orders at earlier stages of delinquency. There was in 1988 no central policy about those who breach conditions of their orders and no formal reporting back to the courts on the results of orders made.

• Specific programmes and 'contracts' for all.

• Individual work, group work, some residential periods and sometimes work with families.

• Most attendance is in the evenings or at weekends except for those being assessed, not attending school, or on holiday schemes.

• Time-limited attendance and reviews of work achieved according to the aims set out in the contracts.

• No difficulties perceived about combining offenders with non-offenders since parents see the centre's work as solving the problem set out in the 'contract'.

• Emphasis on professionally qualified staff but extensive use of volunteers.

• Strong links with the community, both to identify appropriate referrals and to slot young people back into community facilities.

- Until 1988 little central monitoring or collection of data, particularly about those attending voluntarily.
- County Standing Conference on Young Offenders established, including prevention in its remit.

7

Youth Work and Volunteers
The Sunderland scene

The Sunderland Youth Development Group (SYDG) was founded in 1983 as a forum for voluntary and paid youth workers 'involved in preventive work with young people'. Its networks included community associations and those working with specific groups like girls and unemployed people. Its prime mover, Alan Dalton, was co-ordinator of Turning Point, a community education centre in Sunderland. As a youth leader in Durham he had discovered the possibilities of joint work with local agencies to fund and meet the needs of young people on the fringes of trouble. He had first applied with a local probation officer for money from the IT Fund to buy two Miror dinghies for use by such a group of young people. Gradually his youth club built a number of projects with the co-operation of the Intermediate Treatment section of social services and grants from the IT Fund. As explained in the opening chapter of this book, the IT Fund is financed by the DHSS, but independently administered by the Rainer Foundation. It was established in 1978 to encourage initiatives in the community to keep young people out of trouble and to act as a bridge between voluntary and statutory provision for them. It considers applications from youth groups if they are sponsored by a local statutory agency as part of the community provision for the area.

In Sunderland the Youth Development Group worked with representatives from the social services, probation and the intensive project for Intermediate Treatment, Milestones, which was set up under the 1983 DHSS initiative to encourage more alternatives to custody and care. How did it define 'preventive work with young people'? It could after all be asked, as it was in the SYDG annual report for 1985–86 by a volunteer and sessional worker who ran a computer group (the equipment bought with £500 from the IT Fund), 'Well, who isn't at

154

risk?' The SYDG in April 1985 defined its preventive work as follows:

A i) Small group work with young offenders and/or those at risk in the opinion of the Youth Worker (paid or voluntary).
ii) Work with individual young offenders or those at risk.
iii) Work which directly or indirectly challenges negative attitudes and behaviour in young people.
B Work which, it can be demonstrated, is young people centred, regardless of whether it is also activity-based or not.
C Work which directly or indirectly diverts potential young offenders and prevents their entry or continuation up the tariff system.
D Work with young people who are not necessarily already known to the statutory bodies.
E Group work which has as secondary objectives aspects of community and social education, acquiring knowledge, skills, experience and confidence.
F Work which offers the opportunity to integrate young offenders and those at risk into mainstream youth work.
G Work in which an effort on behalf of group members and staff is made to evaluate commitment and development.
H Work which can be seen to be of benefit to the community.

The SYDG went on to explain that this definition allowed it to develop a style of work, support and resources for all those working with young people, whether full-time, part-time or on a voluntary basis. The next logical step in its development would be to employ a full-time worker to help set up new projects, support existing projects and liaise with all those in the area involved with young people at risk. So far funds for such a post had not been forthcoming. Members of the SYDG resented the comparative ease with which they felt funds could be obtained for work with identified offenders who were at risk of custody, and argued that if more resources were devoted to early diversion from offending, a great deal of money and trouble would be saved later.

Many of the aims and activities listed by the SYDG are similar to those of Intermediate Treatment groups for young people at risk run by social services, as in Berkshire, or even those of projects which are alternatives to custody: work to prevent offending through social education, acquiring skills, experience and confidence, with eventual integration into mainstream facilities. But what about the way young people join projects run by members of the SYDG, the structure of the work and the methods used? If they reflected what happens in statutory provision for

Intermediate Treatment, with official referrals, set goals for each individual, contracts, reviews and evaluations, they would turn upside down the principles of voluntary attendance and self-determination which characterize youth work. Youth clubs are generally open to all who are eligible by age, location or interests. Members do not join for a specific period. They come and go as they please and the activities stem from their interests and demands rather than the orders of people who make them attend. Eventually they cease to attend when they and their friends grow beyond the provision of the club.

The restricting factor on this principle of openness and self-determination is that the young people have to obey the rules of the establishment. Those who see the social contract, with duties and rights for everyone, as the basis of a democratic society, have no difficulty about accepting the need for such rules, especially if they are collectively agreed and can be modified. However, critics of the youth services see youth work in general as authoritarian, trying to fit young people into a mould of compliance of which their elders approve, taking them off the streets where their presence is a threat to the bourgeoisie and inculcating goals of middle-class citizenship. Why else would they want to compete for a Duke of Edinburgh award or join the approved activities and learn skills which will make them fit better the roles they have been assigned in a capitalist system?

Writers like Bernard Davies in *The State We're In* (National Youth Bureau Occasional Paper 21, 1981) and *In Whose Interests?* (National Youth Bureau, 1979) have argued that Britain has an undeclared youth policy. There has been a shift of resources over recent years away from non-directive youthwork towards work which tries to modify the behaviour of young people. Thus funds have been made available for intensive Intermediate Treatment to make young people accept the social system and for Youth Training Schemes to adapt them for the labour market. On the other hand, the youth services have been starved of money. At present local education authorities under the 1944 Education Act may support youth services in their areas but there is no statutory obligation on them to do so. Provision is accordingly patchy and consistently underfunded.

In addition, youth workers may think of themselves as non-controlling but they are often linked in the minds of less conformist young people with other figures of authority like teachers. In 1979 Paul Corrigan, a sociologist, wrote a revealing study of attitudes among 14 and 15 year-old boys at two Sunderland schools. Over two-thirds of those interviewed for

Schooling the Smash Street Kids (published by Macmillan Education), when asked why they went to school replied either because they had to, because it was the law, or 'to muck teacher about'. Fewer than a quarter went because they wanted to learn or because they thought it good. They saw teachers as distant figures, just doing a job and often hitting them at random. Youth clubs were sometimes useful as places to shelter from the rain or for their facilities but they sensed that the workers had a mission to change them: 'They keep telling you what to do and "that ain't fair" '.

The SYDG has set as its target young people who are not in mainstream youth clubs, and are not succeeding at school, the younger brothers and sisters perhaps of the Smash Street kids. As 'challenging negative attitudes and behaviour' may well entail pointing out 'that ain't fair', how do the various projects manage their work? In an annual report of the SYDG, Isabel Atkinson explained how the Oxclose and Neighbourhood Youth Project, working from a community school, was acquiring greater skills. The school is also an adult education centre, a community centre, a resource centre and an advisory and training centre for the area. In one week taken at random during 1986 to 1987 there were 111 activities, from groups of young mothers to projects for the unemployed, taking place on the premises of Oxclose Community School. In addition to the pupils at the school, there are regularly 2,000 people using the facilities any week. 'It is particularly important,' she said, 'in the context of the community school of which the project is a part, that young people perceive themselves as at least partly in control of their respective futures.' It was sometimes possible 'to create a diversionary impact without the awareness of the young person concerned' but more often 'a contract is negotiated between the young person and youth worker'. The use of the word 'contract' is perhaps more accurate here than in projects with young offenders on court orders, since the agreement has no element of compulsion.

In the year under review the young people involved in the Oxclose and Neighbourhood Youth Project (ONYP) had enjoyed a range of activities including canoeing, renovating a sailing dinghy, skiing and screen printing. Help from the IT Fund, the Sports Council and the local Youth Advisory Committee which existed at that time had enabled ONYP to buy a small fleet of canoes with appropriate safety accessories and a road trailer. The equipment was regularly used by other youth groups throughout the borough. At ONYP they placed particular emphasis on work with girls: 'They illustrate their needs in different ways from boys, are treated differently by the statutory care services and the juvenile justice system. They are, however, equally at risk in the community and can just as well be served by participation in groupwork programmes.' Accordingly the workers devoted effort to contacting girls at risk and also to retaining their involvement.

The various groups of seven to ten young people – it has been said that the definition of a group in a youth club is the maximum number that can be fitted into a minibus – usually met with one professional youth worker and one volunteer who often had special skills in an activity they were undertaking. The ONYP employed one Area Youth Worker. She was based at the school, with salary paid by the local education authority, part of the establishment of the Education Department Youth and Community Service but responsible to the Deputy Head (Community) of Oxclose School. In addition, the ONYP used for 20 sessions each week 11 part-time staff and five or six volunteers at any one time.

Thus Sunderland Education Department met the cost of salaries and the use of the school premises for the ONYP. The original capital investment for Oxclose School had been made by the local education authority, local church organizations and the Washington Development Corporation. To protect the investment for community use, the school was established by Trust Deed giving, among other benefits, right of access to the community and creating a management committee to govern community use and community initiatives emanating from the school. The trustees of the Oxclose School Management Committee were the Borough of Sunderland, Durham Diocesan Board of Finance and the Washington Development Corporation (which by 1988 had ceased to exist). The Management Committee found funds for the ONYP and other projects from its own nominal charges to users of the premises and from public and private grant-making organizations.

The post of Area Youth Worker at the ONYP is one of four funded by the local education authority Youth Service. Most of its provision is for formal youth clubs, operating on one or two nights a week for the 14–17 year-old age group. It employs over 200 part-time youth workers and caters predominantly for boys, with no stated provision for work with girls, ethnic minorities or young people at risk. The overall budget for youth and community work in the borough was approximately £1.2m in 1988 but this included community associations, salaries, running costs, work based on projects, as well as grants to voluntary organizations like the Turning Point Community Education Centre for the unemployed, which received £35,000 a year. There is little formal contact at management level between Sunderland Youth Development Group and the Youth Service but 90 per cent of SYDG members are local education authority staff and the SYDG receives about £250 a year in grant-aid from the local education authority for project work.

The principle on which the Oxclose Neighbourhood and Youth Project operates is that there has to be a variety of provision within the area to meet the informal educational needs of young people. There can be no set formula and programmes may come in different forms, in different places, at different times and for different needs and groups. Although they aim primarily at those aged over 14, they include children of over ten years of age. There is no upper age limit to involvement in the Project and several adult volunteers, some of whom took part as young people, join in the activities and the decision-making. The kind of young people they are hoping to involve are those frequently discriminated against in society, those not catered for by other agencies, those considered 'undesirable' by society at large, and those who are not members of other youth organizations.

An important difference between the ONYP and most mainstream youth groups is the attention paid by workers to those they perceive as being particularly in need. For example, they follow up non-attendance and find out the reasons why a young person has become disenchanted with the group or does not participate fully. Where possible they try to offer alternative or additional involvement in the Project. But they are quick to point out that the ONYP does not create ghettos of young people at risk, since young people participate only because they want to and some join through personal interest in the particular activities offered.

The policy statement of the ONYP, which is responsible to the Oxclose School Management Committee, states categorically that it is not an agency of control. It seeks to nurture the independence of young people, often working with groups of friends who have come together naturally, strengthening these in order that the young people may benefit from their friends' contributions as well as from their own and those of the staff. They promote positive attitudes like non-violence and co-operation, and tackle common prejudices like racism and sexism, by informal discussion when the opportunity arises through conversation, by their reactions when challenged, and by the way activities and expeditions are planned and undertaken.

On the vexed question of discipline, the ONYP has very few rules. If there is a disagreement about ways in which people should behave, the matter is discussed. Staff are not automatically right because they are staff and they are ready to look at how their responses may have affected the situation. 'We tread a fine line between giving the kids what they want and giving them access to what we want them to have', says the policy statement. It is clear that the hidden agenda is very similar to that in formal, structured groups giving Intermediate Treatment but the method of delivery is totally different.

The method is particularly interesting in the context of Sunderland. Paul Corrigan for his study asked whether the trouble young people got into on the streets was deliberate, a reaction to their sense of being powerless in school and unable to shape their own futures. He found in fact that law-breaking was not usually planned but just happened. The young people would be hanging round the streets 'doing nothing' when someone would have 'a wierd idea' like smashing some milk bottles or throwing stones at windows: 'We have a scrap. It's good fun'. They hung round the streets because they rejected the regimentation of youth clubs and could not afford to pay for commercial amusements. Many lived on isolated estates with poor public transport where vandalism was normal. Nearly a decade later, in June 1987, on Town End Farm Estate there were 263 empty flats, many with their windows smashed and boarded up and their doors kicked in. No one wanted to take the accommodation in an area where the unemployment rate as a whole was the highest in England and Wales (14.6 per cent in June 1987) and which on the estate was as high as 50 per cent. The centre of town was four miles away and it was two miles to the nearest GP's surgery.

If young people have a casual attitude to street vandalism and violence, using force to get what they want, their law-abiding elders also believe in toughness. The population of Sunderland, as of many areas, is ageing, with 13 per cent estimated to be over 65 in mid-1986. It is an area with few people from ethnic minorities. The overall number of young people in the population is diminishing and the reduction is reflecting in court lists, although in one area, Washington, the youth population is still growing. Of those who appeared before the juvenile courts during 1986 in the Sunderland area (which includes Washington and Houghton-Le-Spring) over 13 per cent received Custodial or Care Orders or were sent to the Crown Court for sentence, and at Houghton-Le-Spring juvenile court on its own 22 per cent, nearly all burglars. Did those figures reflect a lack of confidence or knowledge among magistrates about alternative measures? Were those writing reports aware of all the facilities in the community that they could recommend?

New strategy in Sunderland

During 1987 Sunderland adopted 'an integrated policy for a range of IT provision'. First, the Milestones project which had been set up under the 1983 DHSS initiative was taken over as a direct alternative to youth custody and detention centre and was called the Juvenile Justice Project. It would serve the courts and other agencies by offering appropriate disposals for juvenile offenders facing custody and work intensively with young people to help them to reduce the seriousness and frequency of their offending. It would take young people under a Supervision Order whether with a requirement for specified activities or a requirement for 90 days Intermediate Treatment. It would offer a day-time programme, making arrangements as necessary with schools or employers. Social services would run the project with one post seconded by the probation service.

Secondly, it was planned to develop a full range of resources to provide appropriate services for children 'at all points in the justice system, to serve the courts, referring agents, and for young people and their families'. The rationale of the strategy was that diversion, in order to be effective, must occur at all points in the system and operate in concert with the rest of the system, since one course of action had repercussions upon others. If, for example, there was too little provision of a preventive nature, young people just beginning to develop a pattern of offending might be sent to Intermediate Treatment projects prematurely and as a result more persistent offenders pushed on into custody.

Who then was to provide that first, preventive intervention, before groups run by social services for identified offenders, to reduce the risk of involvement in crime? 'The general principle', according to a policy document prepared in 1987 on children's services in Sunderland, 'must always be that of harnessing community resources before committing the scarce resources of the Department.' To that end it recommended that all voluntary youth organizations and development groups, 'particularly those involved with provision of resources obtained through Intermediate Treatment funding', should be vigorously encouraged to continue their efforts to provide preventive activities. A directory of local youth and community facilities should be compiled and issued to all social services and probation area offices.

The directory, circulated in October 1987, explained that a wealth of youth and community facilities existed within the Borough of Sunderland 'which if used to their full potential can also operate as part of a successful delinquency management policy providing very efficient means of "preventing" a young person's inclination towards delinquency and crime'. Intervention at this level would be of a voluntary nature offering 'structure and opportunity in the use of leisure within an established social environment.' The majority of youth organizations listed – there was a section, for example, called 'uniformed groups', of organizations like the Guides and the Boys' Brigade – would seek to cater for a broad cross-section of young people and should not change their approach or atmosphere to accommodate 'the delinquent'. However, some of the facilities listed were more able, adept and willing to work with young people in trouble. The introduction ended on a note of caution: 'It is imperative that whenever young people are referred on a voluntary basis to any of the facilities listed, the term Intermediate Treatment must not be invoked. It would not only be a misuse of the term but could have significant incriminations [sic] if the same young person was later involved in judicial proceedings.'

The Sunderland strategy thus made a distinction between specified tasks carried out within time limits by Intermediate Treatment projects and the open-ended work of youth groups joined on a voluntary basis. It was important to match the young person with the right resource for his or her needs and interests, and the directory emphasized that co-operation between youth leaders and professional supervisors was desirable. The responsibilities imposed on youth groups, which through the support of statutory agencies receive financial help from the IT Fund, were also stressed and the directory included a section on the work of the Fund.

How easy is the relationship between youth groups and statutory agencies? Once they have accepted financial help, either at local level from the local authority or at national level from the IT Fund with local statutory support, can such groups remain untrammelled? Everyone, it seems, agrees that it is their independence from officialdom which helps to make them acceptable to the unclubbable, yet there is sense in their sharing their knowledge of how to help such young people with others. The report of 1985 of the Sunderland Juvenile Crime Consultative Group (one of ten such consultative groups set up under a project funded by the Government and serviced by NACRO) commented that the behaviour of juveniles within the community was often well known to youth workers. 'However, even when this contact is known youth workers are seldom asked to contribute to the preparation of a social inquiry report. However, it is frequently the youth workers who continue to work with the young offender after a court appearance, or a term in custody, without being involved in outlining plans for working with the juvenile within the community.' The Group in its conclusions recommended consultation with the youth service and relevant voluntary organizations to discuss cases coming to court as well as the development of suitable facilities for young people in areas where they were at risk.

In 1985–86 the IT Fund made 42 per cent of its awards to projects 'which might be described as either general youth work resources or community groups', so the situation in Sunderland is not untypical. Most of the grants for the 243 projects the IT Fund monitored in the year had been made to support programmes centred on activities, from sports to computers, although many of the projects also included counselling, community service or groups to solve problems. Writing in the IT Fund's broadsheet *Update*, Alan Dalton discussed the relationship between statutory and voluntary workers. He said that in terms of professional ethics youth workers were reluctant, if not unable, to adopt the 'leave them alone and they will sort themselves out' philosophy, if young people were abusing themselves and others.

An example of the group in Sunderland which in 1987 had been working for two years with young people referred by the probation service, after coming to the notice of the police, or by social services, because of family problems, was the North West Contact Group. It had been set up primarily for those at risk of solvent abuse but it also accepted young people who did not fit into ordinary youth clubs because they were loners or considered disruptive. The group was limited to a maximum of ten at any time so that the workers could get to know each member individually and avert conflict between members. In the course of the group's life only one young person had again been in trouble with the police. The young people were now much less disruptive than when they joined, which posed the problem of whether they should continue with the group or move on. If the group remained static it would become just another youth club which was not its purpose. The group was run by a qualified youth worker with two volunteers. Her post was funded through the grant aid of Turning Point, the centre for the unemployed, and the project also had a grant from the IT Fund.

Ruby Metcalfe, the youth worker, described the work of the volunteers in the 1985–86 annual report of the Sunderland Youth Development Group. The older one, John, helped to organize the activities and had quickly been accepted by the group and gained their confidence. Mark, the younger one, had himself been a member of the original group but now could be relied on to take responsibility. 'Without the help of these volunteers', she said, 'I doubt if this group could run as smoothly as it does.'

In general, volunteers in Sunderland range from young people like those in the North West Contact Group, to parents of children in clubs, to individuals willing to pass on their skills. Volunteers were in 1987 the mainstay of the Tiddlers, a group of about 21 young people aged between eight and 14 who met twice a week to go fishing. The fishing was competitive, with trophies awarded at the end of the year on the basis of one point for each fish caught. Most of their parents were unemployed so could not provide money for equipment. The IT Fund had enabled the purchase of a VHF radio telephone and an echo sounder, equipment for sea fishing from boats. Sunderland is by the sea but it is on a windswept part of the coast and without any equipment the opportunities for using the sea for sport and leisure are limited.

Sometimes it was volunteers who initiated projects. The Town End Farm Junior Youth Project was established in a community centre with a grant from the IT Fund. The volunteers had noticed that there was no provision in the area for those under the age of 14 who used to roam the estate, bored and with nowhere to go. 'It became obvious that it was only a matter of time before they became involved in anti-social activities – indeed, the evidence of petty vandalism, solvent abuse and fire lighting was increasing.' Over 60 young people attended the opening night of the club, which then met weekly, and attendance rarely dipped below 45. As a result, the organizers went on to arrange a play scheme for the summer holidays. This was an example of a general, preventive service for young people developed within the community by community initiative. It became part of the Town End Youth Project, an umbrella organization of voluntary groups and clubs for those aged from seven to 21 on the estate.

Key features

We have seen that in every area considered in this book provision of facilities for young offenders and those at risk is constantly developing. Sometimes planners change the overall framework but the individual components that make up the whole are also frequently modified. The strength of youth groups lies to a large degree in their flexibility, so it is dangerous to generalize about the features of the many organizations working for young people at risk in the community in Sunderland. However, it is fair to summarize thus far:

• Sunderland has a spread of independent ventures in the community which attract, or are set up in order to attract, the kind of young people who do not usually join youth clubs and who are a risk, whether to society (through delinquency) or to themselves (through solvent abuse, drugs, drinking or other behaviour that damages their prospects in life).

• They are based on local communities, often starting from natural friendship groups.

• They have few formal rules and there is maximum participation by members in choosing and running activities.

• Sometimes their membership is open to all, on the lines of conventional youth clubs; sometimes it is aimed at specific groups (like girls) or those with specific interests (like fishing or computers) or those with problems (like solvent abuse).

• They use local volunteers to work with and befriend young people as well as professional workers.

• The local education authority pays salaries for some professional staff but they are otherwise funded by the community with help from the IT Fund.

• There is a local co-ordinating forum for youth workers with representatives from social services and probation but not the education service.

• They operate in an area with a high rate of custody and care for young offenders.

• They are recognized by the statutory authorities as the first stage for preventive work with young people at risk.

• Some groups take referrals from statutory agencies and liaise about progress but without official recording or reporting back.

• There are no official links with the juvenile justice system and offending is not the main focus of groups.

• Neither the groups nor others use the term 'Intermediate Treatment' to refer to their work.

8

The Pattern for the Future

It is clear that different patterns of provision in the community for young offenders and those at risk of offending, whether or not called Intermediate Treatment, have developed partly by accident and partly by design. We have seen from the areas described in this book how a scheme which is an alternative to custody or care can be introduced, where there was previously no provision, to form part of the continuum of care planned by the local authority for children and young people. Another scheme can be brought on financial grounds to fit the existing pattern or organization which may not have been planned to meet the needs of all young people. There is an element of tradition in the way each area reacts to the challenge posed by the deeds and needs of the young, and the political complexion of a place may be less relevant than its traditional ways of responding to young people and organizing services. The left can be as authoritarian and punitive as the right.

It is more complicated to achieve nationwide consistency in juvenile justice than might at first be thought. Like equality of opportunity, it is not an ideal which can be achieved by any single action. There is no simple solution obtainable by imposing rules, certain penalties for certain offences. A few days in any court demonstrate that every offence as well as every offender is different. So is every disposal in the community. The descriptions in this book have shown that although there are common elements in projects aimed at similar groups, varying programmes offer a range of tactics to meet the requirements of those under Supervision Orders and other young people.

Such pluralism in the practice of work with young offenders and those at risk is healthy, giving standards for comparison, enabling choice and development. Diversity of provision through the contribution of voluntary agencies is in a similar way stimulating and constructive. The goal for a fairer and more effective system to tackle offending by young people will not be achieved by a uniform pattern of response, but by a comprehensive spread in every area of complementary resources. Different facilities have to be available at many junctures, times and levels to create a network of supportive services which can divert young people from crime as well as react to their offences. Prevention is part of the cure.

A child care policy

How can such a network of services be achieved, with each contributor having clear goals and working in concert with others? From the areas studied here and from more widespread research, it is plain that the first requirement must be for the services for young offenders and those at risk to be embedded in the area's general child care policy and planning.

Until the early 1980s few local authorities actively shaped policies for children and young people. They reacted to the demands made on them (as it was their duty under Section 1 of the 1933 Children and Young Persons Act to prevent children being received into care) but there was little analysis of what they were doing. When it was discovered just how many children were growing up in local authority care without the security of parents and family,[1] local authorities began to develop child care policies which would ensure that children were either restored to their own families or found new families. The declared aim was to support children and young people in the community and to provide facilities in the community to meet all their needs, preventing reception into care as well as enabling families to come together after a break, if that was in the best interests of the children.

A positive child care policy, such as is now established in many areas, should specifically include young people at risk of offending and young offenders. The 1969 Children and Young Persons Act was never fully implemented but it remains the basis of legislation concerning young offenders. Its underlying tenet, that it is impossible to split each young offender into two separate people, the delinquent and the deprived, has never been overturned, even if it has been modified, often through fears that excessive attention to welfare may be contrary to natural justice. Each aspect of the young person has to be considered, as the successful projects for serious offenders show, addressing both the offence and the individual. The relationship between groups and centres for young people at risk and those on projects aiming to change the behaviour of serious offenders is similar to the relationship between the services which aim to prevent families from breaking up and those which offer children substitute families when necessary. They should be part of a single strategy or continuum of services.

Inter-agency co-operation

An overall strategy for children and young people entails a range of services, not all of which will be provided by any one agency. Inter-agency co-operation and a multi-disciplinary approach to the needs of young people are essential requirements of such a strategy. The DHSS 1983 initiative to increase the number of projects offering alternatives to custody and care encouraged this approach, and it is a feature of areas like Northamptonshire and Basingstoke which now aim to treat all young offenders in the community. The experience of multi-agency groups was found to be favourable in the review *Juvenile Crime: Co-ordination and the Community*, published in 1986 by NACRO. It described the Juvenile Consultative Groups set up in ten areas through a project funded by the Government in 1982. The main tasks of the Groups, most of which continued in some form after the experimental period, were to collect and analyse information about juvenile offending and the system, and to encourage community-based initiatives for young offenders and those at risk.

The co-operation of the social services, the education services, the youth services, the probation services, the police and those who work in the courts, the voluntary as well as the statutory sector, and ethnic minority and community groups, is essential at all stages. Their collaboration is necessary, first to acquire the facts on which decisions can be made. One of the many enduring contributions to an understanding of juvenile offending made by Professor Norman Tutt, Dr Henri Giller and their colleagues at Lancaster University and those at Social Information Systems, is their insistence on the collection, monitoring and evaluation of statistics about the juvenile justice system. Factual knowledge is essential for both planning and advocacy. We have seen how complicated it is to measure the 'success' of Intermediate Treatment or even to monitor rates of re-offending in a way that is helpful. It may even be naïve to attempt to consider the results of social work in this way. Similarly, it is extremely difficult to calculate exactly the costs of different responses to offending. More is involved than just the running costs of a particular programme, as is clear from the work so far on the relative costs and cost-effectiveness of Intermediate Treatment and its alternatives by Martin Knapp and his team at the Personal Social Services Research Unit of Kent University.

However, the basic facts, which can be collected with comparative ease once a system has been established, particularly with the aid of computers, can help to plan provision and to give all those who make decisions an overall view of what is happening in their area. If more facts were routinely collected about the characteristics and circumstances of individual offenders, it would be easier to evaluate the effect of different methods of work with young people, building on the findings of the Cambridge Delinquency Study by D. J. West and his colleagues.[2]

A juvenile liaison panel – an agreed name for bodies which have similar co-ordinating functions would be helpful – is also essential when planning policies for diversion. As was pointed out by many participants in this study, the practices of one part of the system seriously affect those of others, so all the agencies must be aware of each others' work. The policy of 'gate-keeping', ensuring that young people do not slip accidentally or prematurely from one type of provision to another, is enabled by such co-operation. But diversion has two sides. It should not be seen merely as a negative policy, introduced to prevent the damaging effects of young people entering the court process unnecessarily, but as a positive strategy to deter them from offending. If the negative side is stressed too much in order to project what is known as systems management, there is a danger of alienating support. The goal appears to be to beat the system rather than to deter offending, and a negative approach sometimes suggests a lack of conviction about the effectiveness of community alternatives.

Cautioning is the first way young people may be diverted from court once they have come to the attention of the police. There have been many calls for consistency in its use and it is surely wrong that in some areas the police give young people repeated cautions for offences that are admitted, and in others only one. Young people in places where only one caution is given have a criminal record at a stage when, if they lived elsewhere, they would still be of good character. The guidelines on cautioning should make it clear that cautions are preferable to court appearances except for persistent offending of a serious nature. Nor should cautions be cited as a matter of course in court or social inquiry reports. As they have been made without the protection of the open, judicial system, it is contrary to natural justice for them to form a kind of preliminary record. This view does not imply that the police put pressure on young people to admit offences and be cautioned, or that magistrates are not capable of seeing the difference between a conviction and a caution, but cautions should be seen as separate from the court process. In this respect the juvenile court lags behind the adult court, where cautions are no longer cited.[3]

To be effective and acceptable, cautioning depends on there being sufficient facilities in the community for young people and their families to use on a voluntary basis. An informal caution by way of a warning on the spot by a policeman at an early stage, or a formal caution before parents later on, may be enough to make some young people change their behaviour; but the most vulnerable, those often with the least able and supportive parents, require positive help to make changes. The repeated use of cautions makes sense when it is linked with a wider system of diversion. Within a multi-agency group the police are aware of the facilities that social services, the youth service, youth groups and others can offer. Knowledge of such facilities should also do much to overcome opposition, such as that voiced by members of the Magistrates' Association, to repeating cautions. In 1987 the Association passed a resolution asking for limitations on repeat cautioning, but this was against the advice of its own Juvenile Courts Committee.

There remains the question of whether the principle is acceptable of an independent multi-agency body, surveying the conduct of young people and planning intervention in their lives and those of their families. Intervention may be suggested on a voluntary basis but the shadow of the court is there as a reminder of the alternatives to not co-operating. In addition, will representatives of youth groups forfeit the confidence of unclubbable loners whom they are trying to attract, if they are seen to be meeting and working with the police? Will all the members of the group be infected by a sense of solidarity which undermines their separate roles?

The power of such co-ordinating bodies has to be recognized but it should be curbed by the balance of its members. There is also every reason to suppose that most parents appreciate the opportunity to receive sensitive, practical help with their children. That has been the experience in different ways of all the projects studied for this book. In Berkshire voluntary arrangements which had set conditions were not seem as an imposition. Some of the projects involved parents to the extent of organizing groups for them to attend. In others, parents joined and helped activities, whether or not their children were attending as a result of a court order. The danger of infringing rights is likely to be greater through not providing a co-ordinated spread of resource for young people in the community than by steering them into new ventures.

An approach of minimal intervention is often advocated for the problems of young people. It is a healthy corrective to those who are sure they knew what life-style everyone else should adopt and it is consistent with the eventual aim of enabling young people to take responsibility for their own actions and futures. It is, however, unhelpful if it conveys the impression that there is nothing that can be done except wait for young people to grow out of any criminal tendencies. We know too little, although current research may soon tell us more, about the effects of the increasing provision of Intermediate Treatment but it is a mistake to think that non-intervention is a neutral stance. Social workers who receive children and young people into care and then wait for the situation to resolve itself, are in fact adding to the unlikelihood of their clients' returning home.[4] It is assiduous work in the first days and weeks that can bring about changes which will enable a return home. In the same way leaving vulnerable young people to their own devices only reduces the number of options they have for change and lessens the likelihood of their coming to terms with schooling or employment. This point is particularly important in a period when the unsuccessful in our society are trapped by their poverty and lack of skills, with few choices they can exercise.

The positive approach raises the financial issue of the number and scope of facilities that are needed to implement an effective preventive service for young people. Early identification of difficulties is essential and support for families, whether there are one or two parents, is needed early. The relationship between general physical, intellectual and emotional development and behaviour is well attested. The diagnostic services start with health, often through the health visitor's remit for children under the age of five as well as through the GP, and then they centre on the school, through child guidance, school welfare and medical services. All of these are stretched beyond their capacities, and communication, let alone co-ordination, between the social, health and education services is rarely good enough, as the history of child abuse in particular shows. Yet access to specialized diagnostic and remedial services is essential both before and after children reach the age when they may come into conflict with the law. The needs of young offenders and those at risk have to be seen in the context of the welfare and education services as a whole. They are not just the responsibility of those involved with law and order.

The Youth Service

The general facilities in the community, starting with groups for mothers and toddlers, continuing through play groups and nursery provision, to after school facilities and clubs for younger school children, and clubs and groups for teenagers, are also in short supply, often organized by a mixture of professional and voluntary effort. It has been noted that at present local education authorities under the 1944 Education Act are empowered to provide youth services if they so wish, but the provision is not mandatory. In early 1988 an attempt was made to give the youth service a firmer legal base through an amendment to the Education Reform Bill.

The clause was first moved by the SLD MP, Paddy Ashdown, but fell, through lack of time. Drafted by the National Council for Voluntary Youth Services, it proposed to make the local authority's duty to provide youth service facilities for young people between the ages of 11 and 21 mandatory. It should be the duty of every local authority 'to assess the need for and secure provision of facilities, outside full-time education and employment, whereby young people may be assisted to discover their own resources of mind and body, to understand the society of which they form part, to have access to information and skills requisite for playing a full part in that society, and to make a contribution to the economic and social life of their community'. The amendment stated that local authorities should take account of all young people in the area and not just members of youth organizations.

However, the simplest way to increase the provision of youth facilities would be for the DES to mount for local education authorities, in partnership with voluntary bodies, the kind of initiative the DHSS did in 1983 for social services departments and voluntary organizations, to increase the number of alternatives to custody and care. A substantial sum of money, comparable to the £15m put up by the DHSS, should be made available by the Government for new schemes for teenagers and younger children at risk in the community, to be started by a voluntary body with the backing of the statutory authority and with the expectation that after the introductory period they would become a permanent part of the area's provision. Such an initiative could transform the youth service, making clear its responsibility to reach out to young people at risk as well as to serve the more conventional.

There are disadvantages in schemes set up for limited periods. Even if it is recognized from the beginning that they will probably continue once the pump has been primed, it can be difficult for their staff to adjust to the lack of job security. Nevertheless, the continuation of all but a handful of the schemes begun under the DHSS initiative shows that this method of funding is an effective way to accelerate change. Is the Government likely to be interested in funding such an initiative? Unfortunately there is not the same political pressure to expand provision for young people in general, even for those at risk, as there was for projects specifically set up to address offending. The connexions are not recognized, and there is not the political will to investigate the proposition that if there were a comprehensive spread of acceptable facilities for young people in the community, the rate of offending might well be slowed. These are points that must be stressed repeatedly until there is action.

Common features

It has been suggested that there can be no single pattern for how to work with young offenders and those at risk of offending. There are, however, certain features which can and should characterize all projects. The first is clarity of purpose, the starting-point for all effective work. We have seen the importance of identifying not only the type of young person for whom the scheme is available but also the aim of every programme and piece of work. It follows that continuing evaluation is necessary to ensure that goals are being met, and that the whole system must be effectively monitored.

Coupled with clarity of purpose, recording, evaluation and monitoring, must be the ability to communicate purpose and findings in a way that is understood by everyone concerned. The exact form of contracts or agreements made at the outset, even their desirability in all cases, may be questioned but they have the immense advantage in more formal settings of concentrating minds on what is happening and why. They emphasize the active role of young people in deciding their own futures and show parents that they have an important role. Subsequently, clear recording of decisions and progress, and communication to all parties, are essential.

173

As far as offenders are concerned, good communication with those who make decisions in court, judges in the Crown Court as well as magistrates in juvenile courts, makes sense. They are unlikely to trust projects about which they know nothing. It is an unending task to keep the courts informed of all developments, as the personnel concerned change frequently but it is a task which must be undertaken. The importance of reports in the decision-making process has been explained. It makes sense for agencies to offer specialist support to those writing reports. Information about the particular project and programme has to be combined with argument about its appropriateness to the individual. This is particularly important if courts are to be convinced of the desirability of repeating orders for reform in the community. A good way to build mutual confidence and to enable magistrates, judges and workers to examine the effects of community alternatives is for projects to report back to courts on the progress of those on court orders.

The final area where good communication is essential is with the other people and agencies in the lives of the young people, from the social workers carrying the responsibility for Supervision Orders on offenders, to the teachers who have the day-to-day contact with young people on the edges of trouble and whose attitudes may be crucial in determining their response. The essential point is that projects for young offenders and those at risk do not exist in a vacuum and must look to the future. What can be achieved in 90 days? Quite a lot if the work is skilled and purposeful, but whatever is achieved will be maximized if it is carefully built on subsequently and the needs of young people seen in total. Compensatory education may still have a place in some projects on a limited basis, especially for those excluded from school and without any current tuition, but the aim must be to integrate school-age children into mainstream provision.

One reason why the work at the Surrey Juvenile Offender Resource Centre is impressive is the scale on which the Centre has tackled the future needs of young people. The Centre addresses offending clearly as the focus of its work but also has means in the community to help young people to find work and accommodation. Similarly, in Kirklees they have tackled the problem of working with ordinary schools to encourage them to improve their capacity to contain and help difficult, disruptive young people. Liaison with schools is also a starting point in Berkshire. An essential role of those working with offenders and young people at risk is to identify features in society which aggravate the problems of the young. They can use their experience to advocate change in the attitudes and working methods of others which may in turn help to prevent young people from opting out and drifting into delinquency.

How much work with parents should be undertaken by projects centred on the needs of young people? The projects described in this book show various ways of involving the most important figures in the lives of young people. One of the advantages of a juvenile liaison panel is the range of contacts made available to help support parents and when necessary to provide alternative sources of shelter and parenting, whether through accommodation schemes or fostering.

A common feature to emerge from this and other studies is that much of the work with offenders and those at risk is done in groups. Partly this is for economic reasons: it is cheaper to cover the same programme with a group than on an individual basis. In principle, however, groupwork is used because it is considered an effective way to approach young people, allowing them to learn from each other, teaching them to tolerate rules and co-operate with others, perhaps enabling them to break with other deviant groups. The versatility of groupwork is demonstrated by examples of it given in this book but it is clear that identified offenders and many of those on the fringes of trouble also need assessment of their problems and potential as individuals, followed by work to diminish the problems and increase the potential.

Casework of this kind is not bought cheaply, even if it costs the tax-payer less than custody. In addition to the running costs of the projects, professional consultants are expensive but often necessary. Nor are volunteers, whose contribution is important and to be encouraged, whether they teach skills or befriend the young, a free commodity. They need training for specific tasks and support. They are often also paid their expenses. The more individual the attention given to each young person, the more expensive it is to provide the service. This is a factor which will affect further development of tracking schemes, as in West Sussex or Kirklees, if they are more than the literal equivalent in the community of custody. In the short term at least, it is a mistake to rely too heavily on financial benefits when arguing for a change to alternatives in the community.

The fundamental questions

It was explained at the outset that underlying this and any other study of Intermediate Treatment is the problem of definition. None of the projects described in this book used the words Intermediate Treatment in its title. The projects which were alternatives to custody and care preferred, as in Surrey, a title which gave a direct description of their work with offenders, or, as in Lambeth and Kirklees, a more open, general title. The section of legislation they used for their work was that requiring specified activities as part of a Supervision Order, so to avoid confusion they preferred to avoid reference to Intermediate Treatment.

The schemes run by the Social Services Department in Berkshire included some young people on Supervision Orders but they were called Centres, with local names. In Sunderland, although the statutory authority saw local youth groups as an important resource, the first line in preventing delinquent behaviour, and although the groups used funding from the IT Fund, it was stressed that the words 'Intermediate Treatment' should not be used to describe their activities. In other areas, however, there are Intermediate Treatment sections in social services departments and they have IT centres run by IT officers.

What has happened is that the term has evolved into a short-hand description of any kind of work with young offenders or those at risk. It is a code phrase, understood in the trade but mystifying to those outside. As a term to promote, in order to mobilize support, it is a millstone. When the DHSS Social Services Inspectorate carries out an inspection of Intermediate Treatment, most people in the Social Services Department know what the inspectors want to see, even if there is no work there called Intermediate Treatment. Its usefulness as a blanket term, however, obscures the harm it does in allowing vagueness about aims. If it is agreed that clear goals are essential for effective work would it not be better to abandon a name that militates against clarity?

Moreover, if the adjective 'intermediate' is taken literally, the term is becoming out of date. The desirable trend is for alternatives in the community to become substitutes for custody and care and not merely staging-posts on the road to imprisonment. By retaining the word 'intermediate' we fuel the assumption that custody and care are inevitable eventually. The other word, 'treatment', stems from a medical interpretation of delinquency rarely espoused today.

The double goal of seeking to work in the community with both offenders and those at risk was built into the original concept of Intermediate Treatment, as we have seen. The experience of intensive projects which are alternatives to custody and care indicates, however, that to be successful they must usually be separate. They must be part of a wider system but they must tackle specifically the needs of those who were not diverted from offending early on and who are now serious offenders. Although they often have the caring characteristics of a welfare agency and help young people gain control of their lives, they are built on the 'justice' model, with a stated, time-limited remit to address the offence. It is surely better to avoid euphemisms, to be honest and to call them what they are – centres for young offenders. There must be reluctance to label young people at any stage but acceptance of responsibility is part of the process of maturing and avoiding criminal behaviour.[5] If alternatives to custody are to replace custody completely, it is self-deceiving not to recognize that young people are sent to such projects for punishment as well as reform.

The number of projects which are alternatives to custody and care has increased through the 1983 DHSS initiative, but there are still areas where they do not exist. The plea in some areas, such as the London Borough of Hackney in 1988, is that the local authority has not the resources to provide them. The question is one of priorities, but the result of not providing projects is disastrous for young people who could be dealt with better in the community than in institutions. Particularly with crimes involving violence, the magistrates concerned are likely to feel that they are neglecting their duty to the public if the disposal is not custodial. Alternatives to custody may cost less than custody, as seen from the figures produced in Surrey, but they are by no means cheap and the money they save belongs to the Home Office rather than to the local authority which has to finance community projects. At source the money all comes from the taxpayer but that argument does not balance the books of local authority social services departments.

So what can be done to ensure that alternatives to custody do exist in every area as separate facilities? The problem is complicated by the fact that the number of teenagers in the population has started to decline and will continue to do so through the early 1990s, reducing the number of offenders likely to be eligible for intensive projects and thereby increasing the expense of providing for them. There are two approaches. The gradualist approach suggests that where there is an accepted, integrated plan for the area, a custody-free zone can be created, as has happened in Basingstoke, to take the example which has been documented best.[6] The more radical route is to strengthen the Criminal Justice Act even further by defining the serious nature of the crimes for which young people may be sent into custody. We have seen that at present interpretations of seriousness vary greatly from place to place, with the result that the clause of the Criminal Justice Act which is

177

intended to restrict the use of custody for juveniles is an Achilles' heel, allowing a wide interpretation of seriousness. If custody were limited as a possibility to the small number of offenders who had used serious violence and were not amenable to alternatives in the community, this loophole would be closed.

The question that then arises is whether this limitation should be introduced before there are comprehensive alternatives to custody in the community. (Similarly, the wisdom is debated of cutting back residential care for children, or for those with mental handicap, before alternative facilities and support services have been developed.) Dr Jerome Miller was faced with this choice as Commissioner of the Department of Youth Services in Massachusetts.[7] In the early 1970s, after trying to improve the nature of the institutions, he and his colleagues closed them. The young offenders were dispersed to a variety of projects in the community, most of which created special programmes which did not exist before. Mayhem did not ensue and it is hard to see why it should have when it is considered that custodial institutions contain young people for only a short time. They are then released back into the community. We know that in the UK 83 per cent of young offenders after youth custody and 68 per cent after detention centre begin re-offending within two years, so the period the public is protected is brief. In France, to take a European example, *centres fermés* ceased to exist after 1978. A policy of no incarceration for juveniles is coupled with an intensive crime prevention programme, including activities organized in summer in the cities to reduce the crime rate among young people.

It was estimated by a NACRO working party[8] that there were about 400 juveniles who presented a 'direct, immediate, physical and substantial threat to the personal security of the public' and who should be accommodated in secure conditions, possibly in regional centres. If other existing provision in institutions were closed, there would be considerable savings to central government from the 4,000 places not used, on 1986 figures, in youth custody and detention centres. At present the Government is like the Roman god Janus concerning juvenile justice. It faces two ways, its Home Office self funding custodial institutions, and its DHSS persona encouraging community alternatives. The saving on accommodating juveniles in custody could help ease conditions in prison for older offenders by releasing buildings and the cash savings would justify increased DHSS expenditure in lieu, to make sure that every area had its project which was an alternative to custody and care. The solution would in essence fulfil the intentions of the 1969 Children and Young

Persons Act, which envisaged community homes instead of dentention centres and the ending of Borstal for juveniles, with all provision for juveniles organized and funded by local authorities.

A simple way to eliminate any latent unease about mixing young people on court orders with those attending projects voluntarily would be to raise from 10 to 14 the age of criminal responsibility. There are several cogent arguments for making this change. Only 6,100 boys and 500 girls under 14 were sentenced in courts in 1986. Forty-two per cent of the boys and 57 per cent of the girls were discharged either conditionally or absolutely, 17 per cent of the boys and 20 per cent of the girls were given Supervision Orders, leaving only 15 per cent of the boys and 17 per cent of the girls punished by fines and 21 per cent of the boys (three per cent of girls) being sent to Attendance Centres.

Fines are a blunt instrument to tackle offending by young people who frequently come from families dependent on state benefits. The juvenile court has to order fines to be paid by parents unless this would be unreasonable in the circumstances of the case.[9] Parents may appear irresponsible and uninterested in controlling their children but they often need help to exercise their authority and regain their parental role. Fining them may aggravate the underlying difficulties by making them resent even more their inability to control their children. As far as the conditional discharge is concerned, the shock of a court appearance may stop some young people from re-offending, but many juvenile courts are less intimidating than the police station where a caution is delivered. If the conditional discharge is used not so much as a threat but as a bargaining tool, to make the child see the sense of keeping out of trouble, others can explain the consequences of offending. Those really at risk need help to resolve their problems, and alternative activities. The kind of guidance given under a Supervision Order is often given by social services projects and youth groups on a voluntary basis. We have seen that structured programmes can be agreed with children and families without the backing of a court order. In addition, the drop in the number of young people in this age-group in the early 1990s is likely to reduce the numbers in court further.

If the age of criminal responsibility were raised, where would that leave the juvenile court? One possibility for consideration is the extension of its jurisdiction at the upper end to include young people until the age of 18. Any age limit is arbitrary but the present one of the 17th birthday for the juvenile court is particularly difficult to justify. The school-leaving age is 16 so the juvenile court is not restricted to schoolchildren. At 17 young people are thought suitable for the adult court but in no other ways are they considered to be adults before the law. They cannot vote, enter a financial contract, or marry without permission, so why should they be treated as adults in court?

The creation of a youth court would have considerable practical advantages for 17 year-olds in addition to more regard being given to their welfare than in the adult court. They could join the projects in the community which are alternatives to custody and care for juveniles. We have seen that the number of juveniles eligible for these is likely to decline because of demographic factors, so there would be room to accommodate those of 17; their inclusion would remove any temptation for the projects to take young people who were not at risk of custody or care, in order to keep numbers sufficiently large to justify funding. Many of the projects already include those who turn 17 in the course of attendance and those of 17 would benefit greatly from the combination of approaches at centres like the Surrey Juvenile Offender Resource Centre. The age extension would give an incentive to probation and social services to develop more formal and informal opportunities for community service for younger clients and generally encourage co-operation between probation and social services in meeting the needs of young offenders.

A change of the age range covered by the juvenile court would also be supported by the overdue establishment of a family court. This would take in the needs of younger children in trouble through parental neglect, and help to remove any stigma of supervision by social services. The organization of courts, like the provision of facilities in the community, must be seen as a whole. The result of both raising the age of criminal responsibility and creating a family court, to cover the jurisdiction of present care proceedings, would be to give England and Wales some of the features of the Scottish system under the 1968 Social Work (Scotland) Act, at least for children under 14. It is a system which is generally admired and which no one plans to change.

The conclusion that emerges is that the name Intermediate Treatment has outlasted its usefulness, but the variety of work it includes must continue. The term is not used directly in legislation so there is no legal difficulty in discontinuing its use. There are, however, two national bodies which immediately come to mind as having the term in their titles. The IT Fund celebrated its tenth anniversary in 1988. Its role in preventive work is well known, but it could be argued that it would be better known if it had a title which was not primarily associated with the juvenile justice system and which could be projected more easily to the general public. The National Intermediate Treatment Federation (NITFed) raises the final crucial question of training.

Training

It is clear from the accounts of projects in this book that those working with young offenders and young people at risk may have a number of roles. They may act as assessors, teachers, counsellors, therapists, advocates, interpreters, brokers, advisers, liaison officers; as agents of authority and as friends; both organizing and delivering services; dealing with young people, parents, other professionals, volunteers in the community, the police, the courts. Who are the workers with the skills and experience to perform many of these functions and where were they trained?

In March 1988 Barry Anderson of NACRO and Wendy Stafford of the West Sussex Institute of Higher Education published the results of a survey they conducted of those who had attended the 1987 NITFed conference.[10] The survey was not a sample of those currently working in this field but of those informed and enthusiastic enough to join their local Intermediate Treatment association and attend the national conference. About half those sent the questionnaire returned it. There are obvious limitations to such a survey and response but its findings about the backgrounds of the workers are consistent with reports in general and what was learned in the six areas studied for this book. More than half of the respondents had social work qualifications, mainly the CQSW (Certificate of Qualification in Social Work), with about 15 per cent trained as teachers and the same proportion with youth and community work qualifications. Two-thirds were men (there were approximately equal numbers of men and women, as it happened, in the projects studied for this book), nearly all were white and three-quarters were based in specialist teams, with only six per cent in area social services teams.

How, if at all, were the skills and experience they brought from their different backgrounds enhanced and adapted to their new specialism? The answer, as we have seen, is on the job. There is no specific first qualification for work with young offenders, although a survey by the Central Council for Education and Training in Social Work (CCETSW) of 2,561 social work students who qualified in 1985 showed that for 24 per cent their first posts had 'a major emphasis' on offenders. At present most social workers have two years of study and practice in order to qualify for the CQSW. Graduates in related disciplines may complete the course in a year and those taking the CSS (Certificate in Social Work) attend college part-time for two or three years while in employment. The prescribed content for courses for the CQSW covers social administration, elements of psychology, sociology, human growth and behaviour, social work theory and practice. Half the course is based in agencies and assessed placements last at least 50 days. The usual approach to the curriculum for both qualifications is through modules on different topics but in such a short time, with so much ground to cover, it is not surprising that there are few modules on juvenile offending. As we have seen, the course can be completed with only the most cursory study of child care law and child development, let alone the theory and practice of work with offenders.

In 1988 the Government rejected the proposal by CCETSW for a new, three-year Qualifying Diploma in Social Work. One of the many hopes which were thereby shattered was for the option of more attention being paid to the needs of young people at risk of offending, not just by those intending to specialize in work with them but by all social workers who in the course of generic work with families are bound to come across children at risk. We have seen that if a genuine preventive system is to be established, as well as one of diversion from the criminal justice system, greater understanding of the issues is needed by all those in contact with young people, from social workers, to teachers, to members of the health profession. The argument for extending social work training must be revived and won.

The only post-qualifying course on work with young offenders considered for approval by CCETSW in 1988 was that run by the West Sussex Institute of Higher Education. There are also short courses, notably those run by Lancaster University's Centre of Youth, Crime and Community, and Masters' courses in criminology, but the gap for most workers is filled by voluntary effort, those who work with young offenders coming together to share their expertise.

The March 1988 issue of *Youth Social Work*, itself an invaluable compilation of information and news 'for those involved and interested in services for young people at risk or in trouble, in social services, probation, youth service, the voluntary sector and allied settings', had reports from 13 national and local organizations offering training on various issues. They ranged from a leaving home project, to the North

West Detached Work Forum, to the National Association of Motor Projects, to five regional IT associations. Their topics and workshops included ones on work with girls, victims, community homes with education, young people on their own territory, housing, social, inquiry reports and child care planning teams.

The extent of this activity is admirable, but it does not compensate for the time and expertise lost through the lack of initial and post-qualification training. It means that most workers in this field will know little specialist theory or, perhaps more dangerous, only aspects of theory relevant to their previous profession. Does it matter if they have never heard of Matza's theories about adolescent groups, cannot trace the influence of Albert Cohen[11] on the development of Intermediate Treatment, are ignorant of Ivan Illich and de-schooling[12] and have not read Edwin Schur on the case for not intervening with young people?[13] Work with young offenders may appear to be mainly practical but it always helps to know why you are adopting a certain course of action.

Certainly, in projects which are alternatives to custody and care, the worker needs understanding, which teachers are taught, of cognitive development and the way people learn; insight into individual and group behaviour which social workers are taught; and some of the skills in handling the young and understanding their backgrounds which are the speciality of youth and community workers. Those who responded to the NITFed questionnaire on qualifications and training identified 67 training needs, with aspects of race most frequently cited. Workers in this field have a special responsibility to meet the needs of minority groups, whether black boys in an area with a low proportion of people from ethnic minorities, or girl offenders who come before the courts less frequently than boys and for whom there are fewer facilities in the community. It takes considerable effort and time for each recruit to acquire what he or she needs on an individual basis, within the constraints of a day-to-day workload and variable funding by employers for staff development.

The West Sussex Institute's Advanced Certificate in Social Work with Young Offenders is for qualified or experienced social workers able to work with young offenders during the course. Christopher Hardy, who founded and leads the course, designed it to combine distance learning, by correspondence, with four residential courses of a week each. The aim is to provide the knowledge and competence to work effectively with juveniles and young adults and to be able to provide a specialist advisory service to colleagues. The main topics of the course include the background and local incidence of crime; social and psychological theories; legislation, guidelines, policy and provision; how to assess, plan and evaluate work; how to develop networks; how to identify areas for improvement in provision and the processes necessary for change in agencies; understanding the legal process. The student works on a programme to develop skills, submits a course paper to show how theory can be put into practice and conducts a project while on a placement. Each project is planned individually to meet the needs of the student and the setting where he or she works. The course began in 1983 and now has about 20 students a year drawn from most areas and backgrounds.

More such courses, stressing practical skills as well as understanding of the system, are clearly needed. Opportunities to work with young offenders and those at risk have increased recently with the creation of new schemes. The argument of this book is that expansion is still needed, particularly of preventive work. Better training is necessary not only to improve the quality and effectiveness of work but also to establish criteria for those making a career in the field.

The training of magistrates has both grown and improved in recent years, with all magistrates now undertaking on appointment a commitment to continuing training. Both in the initial training for those joining juvenile panels and in regular training meetings there should be emphasis on explaining the nature and importance of disposals in the community, with frequent visits to local projects. Joint training of magistrates and practitioners can be extremely enlightening on many topics of mutual interest, from local patterns of crime to child abuse.

In the end, the effectiveness of work with difficult, vulnerable young people depends on the abilities and resources of the workers, within the planned framework that has been suggested. Knowledge and skills can and must be boosted but it takes a mature personality to be comfortable with the number of roles that have to be accepted. If there is a single fallacy confusing thought about juvenile offending, it is that there is a single quick cure for it. The public find it hard to accept that the causes of delinquency are complex, affected by society as well as individual actions. Magistrates are disappointed if a Supervision Order is not effective in stopping offending and have to be persuaded to repeat the medicine. Similarly, those working with young people who are in trouble or at risk have to be able to take a long view of their work.

All the projects visited for this study were asked the same questions from a semi-structured questionnaire. One of the topics covered was the training necessary to work with young people. Interesting discussions ensued everywhere on this point but one worker, a former teacher, wrote afterwards: 'Having talked to you last week I've been thinking about what it is that is needed to work in the area of Intermediate Treatment in particular and social work in general. I don't think that it is so much teaching ability but rather something John Keats the poet described as negative capability.' It is that capacity to have faith, to hold on when the outcome is uncertain, to concentrate on the immediate work, to know that it may not be possible to prove that any one course of action will make everything right, which is needed by all who work with young offenders and those at risk.

Proposals for change

The proposals for change made in this final chapter will not please everyone. They are likely to be opposed on the one hand by those who want to deal firmly with juvenile offending and believe, for example, that custody is the right response from society to young people who are persistent burglars of other people's homes. It is to be hoped that the descriptions of projects in this book will help to convince them of the toughness and comparative effectiveness of measures in the community. Others will object to the amount of intervention countenanced here in the lives of young people and their families, albeit on a voluntary basis. They will say it masks social control under a liberal mantle. Both groups may cavil at the amount of discretion given to multi-agency groups without the checks accorded through the judicial process.

The arguments in reply have been stated but it should be repeated in conclusion that the policies favoured here, many of which are not new, are empirical and practical as well as idealistic. They are based on the experience of the last decade and on growing evidence that measures in the community at every stage are the best way to enable young people both to follow their own paths as individuals and be law-abiding members of the community. Juvenile offending should not be discussed in isolation but should be considered in relation to the conditions in which young people grow up and the attitudes of society.

It can be misleading to summarize, item by item, proposals which are complex and have to be seen in relation to each other and the general argument, but it may be helpful to list some of the main points:

• Planning for young offenders and those at risk to be part of each local authority's stated child care policy.

● Each area to have a juvenile liaison panel with representatives from social services, probation, education, the youth services, the police, the Crown Prosecution Service, the magistracy, justices' clerks, statutory agencies and voluntary organizations in the community. The panel should collect and share information about the way the services operate and are used, identifying gaps and encouraging participation by the community.

● Each area to have both an alternative project to custody or care and a spread of provision offering preventive services, with access to specialist assessment and remedial services. The target group for each facility should be clear.

● An initiative to increase youth service provision and the number of youth groups should be launched, similar to the 1983 DHSS initiative to increase alternatives to custody and care, with special emphasis on reaching those at risk.

● Projects to which courts send young offenders should have the clear aim of addressing the offending behaviour; good communication and liaison; stated aims and conditions agreed with all concerned; careful monitoring, evaluation and reporting back; and should build bridges in the community for the young person to use afterwards. The expansion of informal forms of community service and reparation schemes should be encouraged. Although some remedial education may be suitable for individuals, the aim should be to integrate young people of school age into mainstream provision.

● Less emphasis should be put on the tariff as a concept and more on the advisability of repeating appropriate measures.

● The Criminal Justice Act should be amended to restrict the custody of juveniles to those who have committed serious crimes of violence. The subsequent savings to the Home Office should be used to the benefit of juveniles.

● The age of criminal responsibility should be raised to 14.

● Consideration should be given to including 17 year-olds in the jurisdiction of the juvenile court.

● Family courts should be introduced.

● With the provision of adequate diversion in the community, the repeated use of cautioning should be presumed to be appropriate for juveniles except for persistent, serious offending. Cautions should no longer be cited in court.

● More emphasis should be given to helping mainstream institutions (like schools, youth clubs and Youth Training Schemes) to interest, contain and take back disturbed and disruptive young people.

- There should be more post-qualification training courses for those working with juvenile offenders and young people at risk and opportunities expanded to study this area in qualifying courses for social work, teaching, and youth and community work.
- More attention should be paid in magistrates' training to explaining the structure and nature of provision in the community for young offenders and those at risk.
- Attention in training and on projects should be paid to the special needs of black young people and girls.
- There should be continuing research about the effects of intervention at all stages.
- The term Intermediate Treatment should gradually be dropped in favour of clearer titles for projects and services.

References

1 ROWE, J., and LAMBERT, L., *Children Who Wait*, ABAA (now BAAF), 1973.

2 WEST, D. J., *Delinquency. Its Roots, Careers and Prospects*, Heinemann, 1982.

3 *Time for Change. A New Framework for Dealing with Juvenile Crime and Offenders*, NACRO, 1987, p. 18.

4 VERNON, J., and FRUIN, D., *In Care: a Study of Social Work Decision-making*, National Children's Bureau, 1986.
MILLHAM, S., BULLOCK, R., HOSIE, K., and HAAK, M., *Lost In Care: the Problems of Maintaining Links between Children in Care and their Families*, Gower, 1986.
DHSS, *Social Work Decisions in Child Care: Recent Research Findings and their Implications*, DHSS, 1985.

5 See the discussion of D. Matza's work in MUNCIE, J., *The Trouble with Kids Today: Youth and Crime in Post-war Britain*, Hutchinson, 1984.

6 RUTHERFORD, A., *Growing out of Crime*, Penguin, 1986, pp. 136–47.

7 ibid., pp. 68–107. MILLER, A. D., OHLIN, L. E. and COATES, R. B., *A Theory of Social Reform*, Cambridge Mass: Ballinger, 1987.

8 Quoted in GIBSON, B., 'The Abolition of Custody for Juveniles – Part II', *Justice of the Peace*, 29 November 1986, p. 758.

9 In 1986 parents paid fines for 35 per cent of children aged 10–14 and for 21 per cent of young people aged 14–16.

10 ANDERSON, B., and STAFFORD, W., 'Recruitment and Training for IT Practitioners', *Youth Social Work*, no. 6, March 1988, pp. 9–11.

11 COHEN, A., *Delinquent Boys. The Culture of the Gang*, Macmillan, 1955.

12 ILLICH, I. D., *De-schooling Society*, New York: Harper & Row, 1971.

13 SCHUR, E., *Radical Non-intervention: Rethinking the Delinquency Problem*, Prentice Hall, 1973.

Selected bibliography

ADAMS, R. *et al.*, *A Measure of Diversion? Case Studies of Intermediate Treatment*, National Youth Bureau, 1981.

BELSON, W. A., *Juvenile Theft – The Causal Factors*, Harper and Row, 1977.

BLACK, H., *Report of the Children and Young Persons Review Group, Belfast*, HMSO, 1979.

BOTTOMS, A. E., 'On the decriminalisation of English Juvenile Courts, in HOOD, R., ed., *Crime, Criminology and Public Policy. Essays in honour of Sir Leon Radzinowicz*, Heinemann, 1974.

BOX, S., *Recession, Crime and Punishment*, Macmillan Educational, 1987.

BURNEY, E., 'All things to all men: justifying custody under the 1982 Act', *Criminal Law Review*, 1985, pp. 284–90. *Sentencing Young People. What Went Wrong with the Criminal Justice act 1982*, Gower, 1985.

CASHMORE, E., and TROYNA, B., eds., *Black Youth in Crisis*, Allen & Unwin, 1982.

CAWSON, P., *Young Offenders in Care*, DHSS, 1980.

COHEN, A., *Delinquent Boys. The Culture of the Gang*, Macmillan, 1955.

CORRIGAN, P., *Schooling the Smash Street Kids*, Macmillan Educational, 1979.

CRAMPTON SMITH, G., and CURTIS, S., *It's Your Life, Laws*, Longman, 1983.

DAVIES, B., *Threatening Youth. Towards a National Youth Policy*, Open University Press, 1986.

DAVIES, B, and GIBSON, A, *Social Education of the Adolescent*, University of London, 1967.

DHSS, *Social Work Decisions in Child Care. Recent Research Findings and their Implications*, DHSS, 1985.

FARRINGTON, D., 'The effects of public labelling', *British Journal of Criminology*, 17, pp. 112–25.

FOUCAULT, M., *Discipline and Punishment – the Birth of Prison*, Allen Lane, 1977.

FREEMAN, M. D. A., *The Rights and Wrongs of Children*, Francis Pinter, 1983.

GILLER, H., 'Is There a Role for a Juvenile Court?', *The Howard Journal*, Vol. 25 No. 3, 1986.

GILLER, H., and MORRIS, A., *Care and Discretion. Social Workers' Decisions with Delinquents*, Burnett Books, 1981.

GOLDSTEIN, J., FREUD, A., and SOLNIT, A. J., *Before the Best Interests of the Child*, Burnett Books/Deutsch, 1980.

HARRIS, R., and WEBB, D., *Welfare, Power and Juvenile Justice*, Tavistock, 1987.

HAZEL, N., 'The use of family placements in the treatment of delinquency', in TUTT, N., ed., *Alternative Strategies for Coping with Crime*, Basil Blackwell, 1978.

HEIMLER, E., *Survival in Society*, Weidenfeld & Nicholson, 1975.

HOGHUGHI, M., *Troubled and Troublesome. Coping with Severely Disordered Children*, Burnett Books, 1978.

HOGHUGHI, M., et al., *Assessing Problem children*, Burnett Books/Deutsch, 1980.

HOME OFFICE, *The Sentence of the Court. A Handbook for Courts on the Treatment of Offenders*, HMSO, 1986.

HOPE, P., *Voluntary Organisations and Intermediate Treatment*, NCVO, 1981.

ILLICH, I. D., *De-schooling Society*, New York: Harper and Row, 1971.

KNAPP, M., *The Economics of Social Care*, Macmillan, 1984.

KNAPP, M., and ROBERTSON, E., 'Has IT proved cost-effective?', in HARRISON, A., and GRETTON, J., eds., *Crime UK 1987*, Policy Journals, pp. 57–64, 1987.

MARSH, P., ROSSER, E., and HARRÉ, R., *The Rules of Disorder*, Routledge & Kegan Paul, 1978.

MARSHALL, T., *Reparation, Conciliation and Mediation*, Home Office Research and Planning Unit Paper 27, 1984.

MATTHEWS, R., and YOUNG, J., *Confronting Crime*, Sage, 1986.

MATZA, D., *Delinquency and Drift*, Wiley, 1964.

MATZA, D., *Becoming Deviant* Prentice Hall, 1969.

MAYS, J. B. et al., *Juvenile Delinquency, the Family and the Social Group*, Longman, 1972.

MCCABE, S. and TREITEL, P., *Juvenile Justice in the UK. Comparisons and Suggestions for Change*, New Approaches to Juvenile Crime, 1984.

MCGUIRE, J., and PRIESTLEY, P., *Offending Behaviour. Skills and Stratagems for Going Straight*, Batsford, 1985.

MILLHAM, S., BULLOCK, R., HOSIE, K., and HAAK, M., *Lost in Care; the Problem of Maintaining Links between Children in Care and their Families*, Gower, 1986.

MILLHAM, S., BULLOCK, R., and HOSIE, K., *Locking Up Children*, Saxon House, 1978.

MORRIS, A., and GILLER, J., *Providing Criminal Justice for Children*, Edward Arnold, 1983.

MORRIS, A., GILLER, H., SZWED, E., and GEACH, H., *Justice for Children*, Macmillan, 1980.

MOXON, D., JONES, P., and TARLING, R., *Juvenile Sentencing: is there a Tariff?*, Home Office Research and Planning Unit Paper 32, 1985.

MUNCIE, J., *The Trouble with Kids Today. Youth Crime in Post-War Britain*, Hutchinson, 1984.

MUNGHAM, G., and PEARSON, G., eds., *Working Class Youth Culture*, Routledge & Kegan Paul, 1976.

NACRO AND SOLACE (Society of Local Authority Chief Executives), *Local Authority Action on Juvenile Crime. A Role for Chief Executives*, NACRO, 1987.

PACKMAN, J., *The Child's Generation*, Blackwell, 1981.

PALEY, J., and THORPE, D., *Children – Handle with Care. A Critical Analysis of the Development of Intermediate Treatment*, National Youth Bureau, 1974.

PARKER, H., CASBURN, M., and TURNBULL, D., *Receiving Juvenile Justice*, Basil Blackwell, 1981.

PEASE, K., and MCWILLIAMS, W., eds., *Community Service By Order*, Scottish Academic Press, 1980.

PERSONAL SOCIAL SERVICES COUNCIL, *A Future for Intermediate Treatment. Report of the Intermediate Treatment Study Group*, 1977.

PITTS, J., *The Politics of Juvenile Crime*, Sage, 1988.

PIZZEY, R., ed., *Intermediate Treatment. An Interventionist Strategy for the Police*, Police Staff College, Bramshill, 1982.

POINTING, J., ed., *Alternatives to Custody*, Blackwell, 1986.

PRIESTLEY, P., FEARS, D., and FULLER, R., *Justice for Juveniles*, Routledge & Kegan Paul, 1977.

PRINGLE, M. K., *The Needs of Children*, Hutchinson, 1974.

RICHARDSON, N., *Justice by Geography? A Review of Six Local Juvenile Justice Systems Monitored by Social Information Systems*, Social Information Systems, 1987.

ROWE, J., and LAMBERT, L., *Children Who Wait*, ABAA (now BAAF), 1973.

RUTHERFORD, A., *Growing Out of Crime*, Penguin, 1986.

RUTTER, M., and GILLER, H., *Juvenile Delinquency. Trends and Prespectives*, Penguin, 1983.

RUTTER, M., et al., *Fifteen Thousand Hours. Secondary Schools and their Effects on Children*, Open Books, 1979.

SCHUR, E. M., *Radical Non-Intervention. Re-thinking the Delinquency Problem*, Prentice Hall, 1973.

SMITH, C., FARRANT, M., and MARCHANT, H., *The Wincroft Youth Project*, Tavistock, 1972.

STANLEY, S., and BAGINSKY, M., *Alternatives to Prison. An Examination of Non-custodial Sentencing of Offenders*, Peter Owen, 1984.

STEVEN, P., and WILLIS, C. F., *Race, Crime and Arrests*, Home Office Research Study no. 58, HMSO, 1979.

STEWART, G., and TUTT, N., *Children in Custody*, Gower, 1987.

STONE, M., *Intensive Intermediate Treatment for Persistent Young Offenders. A Study of the Junction Project*, University of Surrey, 1984.

THOMAS, D., *Principles of Sentencing*, Heinemann Educational, 1979.

THORPE, D., SMITH, D., GREEN, D., and PALEY, J., *Out of Care. The Community Support of Young Offenders*, Allen & Unwin, 1980.

TUTT, N., *Managing a Diminishing Problem. Background Paper for Association of Directors of Social Services Conference*, Social Information Systems, 1986.

VERNON, J., and FRUIN, D., *In Care. A Study of Social Work Decision-making*, National Children's Bureau, 1986.

WEST, D. J., *Delinquency. Its Roots, Careers and Prospects*, Heinemann, 1982.

WILSON, H., 'Parental supervision, a neglected aspect of delinquency', *British Journal of Criminology*, 20, pp. 203–5.

WILSON, H., and HERBERT, G. W., *Parents and Children in the Inner City*, Routledge & Kegan Paul, 1978.

WILSON, J., *Practical Methods of Moral Education*, Heinemann Educational, 1972.

WOOTTON, B., *Crime and Penal Policy*, Allen & Unwin, 1978.

Index

193